HAVE
BABY
WILL
TRAVEL

HAVE BABY WILL TRAVEL

SARAH TUCKER

Illustrations by
PAM WILLIAMS

Lennard Publishing

First published in 2000 by
Lennard Publishing
a division of
Lennard Associates Ltd
Mackerye End
Harpenden
Herts AL5 5DR

A catalogue record for this book is available
from the British Library.

ISBN 1 85291 143 3 (paperback)
ISBN 1 85291 144 1 (hardback)

Cover design: Paul Cooper Design
Front cover photograph: John McLellan

Printed and bound in Great Britain by
WBC Book Manufacturers, Bridgend

CONTENTS

For Tom

AUTHOR'S ACKNOWLEDGEMENT

Where do I start? Big thank you to my husband, for giving me Tom, to my family – and especially to my father who never met Tom but who I know would have adored him more than anyone and is watching over him now.

To Adrian, Gina and Petra for believing in the idea, Alastair and Patricia for believing in me and starting me in travel reporting in radio and TV respectively, Nim for introducing me to Canada, Revel and Patricia for giving me the break of a lifetime by allowing me (after much pleading) to film in the Yukon five months pregnant and to Brian, Peter, Sheera, Randy and Cliff for being such a fun and talented crew.

Thank you to ray of sunshine Jane for helping me to make the Jazz FM radio show happen.

To my very dear and extremely tolerant friends – a lot of whom seem to be called Claire or Clare, or Karen or Carron for some reason. Add to that Amanda, Anna, Christine, Fiona, Helen, Judith, Susan, Suzanne, Zarina – and especially Caroline.

To Pam for the excellent illustrations.

To all the very stimulating people I have met on my travels and especially to those who have allowed me to mention them in this book.

Lastly, a big thank you to Coline for always being so supportive.

Special thanks to Roger for introducing me to Jazz – and to the best producer in the world (or at least in the UK) Chris (and his brilliant wife Sarah) for producing such a polished show, despite working with an unpolished presenter. To all the team of correspondents who have been so creative from the start. Especially Peter and Chris.

PROLOGUE

Tom is completely wonderful. I didn't plan to have him and I admit his arrival was less than convenient. My job as a radio journalist meant I had to get up and go at short notice, frequently with only hand luggage, tape recorder and passport. It is a wonderful job and I didn't want to give it up.

So, on discovering I was pregnant, I spoke to friends who were already mothers. Most had rarely ventured out of their own town within the first 12 months. Yet, looking back, they regretted the confinement. They acknowledged that it was a lack of confidence and information that had kept them so close to home.

I wanted to see my baby grow up but I also wanted to continue my travels. Could I do both?

I asked people who regularly travel long distances with their families – expatriates, who are forced to travel through their work. They all said the same thing. The easiest time to make such a journey with a child is in its first year. Young babies eat and sleep, they don't crawl, walk, or answer back, and they don't run up and down the aisle of the plane.

So after Tom was born in December 1998, I decided to investigate for myself the pros and cons of travelling with a very young baby to different countries. In particular I wanted to return to those countries I had visited as an independent traveller. In this book I compare the differences of the visits to each country.

I also include comments from some of the celebrities I have interviewed for the radio show which I present on Jazz FM every week – their anecdotes about travelling with babies, and their helpful tips.

SEX ON STILTS

Tom was born on 20 December 1998. I didn't want a Christmas baby. I didn't want to call my son or daughter Holly or Noel. I live in Essex, land of the flat landscape and vowel. Names were easy if it was a boy: Thomas or Edward or Benjamin. Names which even when shortened wouldn't sound too bad – Tom, Ed, Ben. Even the worst could only be Tommy, Eddy, Benny.

A girl would be more difficult. I liked Charlotte and Megan. My partner liked the names of his ex-girlfriends. We couldn't agree, but it would probably be Charlotte. One of my ex-boyfriends had an old classic car which he called Lottie. I liked the car and had fond memories of the ex, so I would be quite happy with Lottie.

I had mixed feelings about being a mother.

I had conceived Tom on Pangkor Laut, a tropical island paradise off the west coast of the Malaysia peninsula. Pavarotti, who described the island as heaven on earth, had formally opened the man-made resort several years earlier. My own expectations of heaven were simpler.

The resort consists of 123 villas by the beach and up in the hills, each with its own verandah and outdoor bathroom. There is an untouched tropical rain forest in the middle of the island which a guide – Mr Yip – will show visitors on a daily tour.

The tour could take a couple of hours if you went by yourself at a steady pace. It would take all day with Mr Yip as he told you what this plant was called, and what that flower could cure, and what that insect did to your libido or lifespan if it bit you. Very interesting no doubt, but in the heat of the midday sun, a lot to take in.

The island also has three restaurants open during the day and six in the evening, all totally relaxed and informal. It helps to like fish on the island of Pangkor Laut but traditional Malaysian and Chinese cuisine are also available.

I had visited the island briefly on a press trip the year before.

I had travelled with a friendly group of journalists on a magnificent tea ship – the Star clipper, which sails between Singapore and

Thailand – stopping off at various islands en route. The Pangkor Laut excursion from the clipper was exclusively for journalists – we were whisked away by speedboat one lunchtime.

Trips specifically designed for journalists tend to be either so full of activities that we literally fly from one interview or meeting to the next without appreciating the surroundings, or there is so much free time, we forget why we're there. In general, travel journalists spend far too much time with the sales managers and managing directors of hotels and restaurants, finding out about how many rooms, bathrooms, boardrooms they have, and not enough time simply looking at the sights and talking to the locals. People don't care how many rooms a hotel has – only that their own room is up to standard and that their air-conditioning is working.

On Pangkor Laut we were shown the luxury suites, which are impressive. Each is beautifully furnished, has a King Kong size bed and an open air bathroom. The only risk you incur on this pleasure island is that a coconut may drop on your head and crush your skull while you sit in the bath al fresco. A small price to pay for paradise.

Though the trip to Pangkor Laut had been brief, I liked what I had seen. So a year later I decided to investigate the cost of returning for about ten days with partner but without press. It would be the first holiday we had had for ages. We were both in desperate need of rest and relaxation and some sunshine. Press trips, no matter how luxurious the destination and well paced the itinerary, are work. Not that I'm knocking press trips: they beat being in an office. I know. I've been there.

So the following March, partner and I set off for Kuala Lumpur from Heathrow. We spent one day in the KL Hilton (strongly recommend it, with or without baby) and after a chauffeur-driven journey to the coast we took a half-hour boat ride to the island. Normally there would be a domestic flight to the coast, but the airport was 'undergoing renovation', and consequently the four-hour journey by car was the only way to get there. The driver was friendly without being pushy and the boat trip passed without incident.

Although I always take work on holiday, for some reason on this one my papers remained firmly in my suitcase. Instead I read several of Bill Bryson's books. Agreed with his views about the Austrians and Austria, the Italians and Italy. Ate salad and fish and rice, drank lots of water and mango juice, slept a lot and got to know and like and appreciate my partner again. It must have been the heady combination of the singing trio performing their unique rendition of Abba's Knowing Me Knowing You and Gimme Gimme Gimme A Man After Midnight, and the Kir Royales that did it. Anyway, Tom was conceived on the island: in a villa on stilts.

MUMMY'S FIRST STEPS

I didn't want to be in hospital, screaming blasphemy on Christ's birthday. I didn't want Tom on 25 December. I wanted Tom to be a Sagittarian, born between 22 November and 20 December. I have never met a Sagi I don't like. They tend to be full of life, extremely tactless, with plenty of get up and go, and are very ambitious and determined. They have a very strong and wonderful sense of fun and make good friends if not good partners. I wanted Tom to be a Sagittarian in the Year of the Tiger, which would make him a right handful but very independent and very lucky. He needed to be lucky having me as a mother.

Tom was due on 17 December according to the doctor's calculation. I still had so much to do and see before the baby arrived. For a start, I was scheduled to go to Canada and present a documentary on the Discovery Channel. The idea was that I would follow in the footsteps of the gold rush prospectors a hundred years after they had made their original journey in search of gold. I was five months pregnant when I went to the Yukon. Tom didn't show (not even a bump), but I hadn't expected quite as much activity filming on location. We went white-water rafting, flew over glaciers and forest fires in an aerobatic helicopter, went fishing with the First Nations, climbed steep hills and walked through long passes. I even danced on stage, high kicking as the show girls had done a hundred years before: all at five months pregnant. I could sense Tom enjoyed it. I loved it.

The last few weeks of pregnancy were the worst, when I was getting heavier and starting, by force of gravity, to slow down. My aerobics instructor, Mark (the only one to keep me sane and in shape the last few months before Tom arrived), was becoming seriously worried that I would give birth in class. But on 18 December, Tom was still happy, kicking and punching. And still in my tummy. I decided to take action. Castor oil, reflexology, an extra strong M & S curry and sex with partner (not all at once or in that order). Contractions duly started on the afternoon of the 18th.

Labour was long and painful. Don't believe what you are told about the pain – the reference books may tell you that it is positive pain. It is not. It is medieval pain. Gas and air is wonderful, an epidural is brilliant.

Tom was born to the sound of the Salvation Army singing Oh, Come All Ye Faithful. I remember the sound quite clearly in between the midwife telling me to pant, to puff and to stop. Tom was calm when he came into the world. There was no shrill cry or even a whimper. He looked at me as if to say, 'Where's this then? Another place, another adventure?'.

This was his greatest and most difficult one; the first of many.

MY HOME TOWN

The First Few Weeks
and How I Met Tom's Father

Chelmsford. The fastest growing town in Europe at the time of going to press, and the county town of Essex. It always seems to be windy and wet there, which doesn't sound very inspiring, does it? I have a house there, where I live with Tom's father.

At least the architects and town planners never made the same mistake twice in Chelmsford. There is only one high-rise block of flats. One concrete multi-storey car park. One Seventies mistake. One killer roundabout and one nonsensical one-way system and one bypass that

doesn't. Everything else is fine. This town has history, culture, a river running through it, its own ornate cathedral, the county cricket ground and Duke's night club.

Duke's night club is famous in Essex. Possibly the club is even talked about in neighbouring Kent and Suffolk. Duke's is a flashing lights, pulsating, brilliant music, heavily mirrored, black and chrome, floor throbbing, smoke filled, rude-named-cocktail sort of place.

I used to visit Duke's with my schoolfriends every Friday night. We went there to dance, not to 'pull'. One Friday night, a guy asked if I would like to see his collection of knives. He said this as though it was a chat-up line, expecting that I would be seriously impressed. I think he believed I was. No, I wouldn't dance with him.

I met Tom's father at Duke's. I had been invited that night because Tom's father worked with my best friend at the time. He fancied her and had invited her to his 21st. I was 23 and already had a boyfriend: my first. Totally oblivious to how un-cool it was to talk about a boyfriend in front of another man, I would tell them how wonderful my boyfriend was, how kind and thoughtful, how intelligent and special. I did not realise that this was the biggest turn-off in the world and that other men would think 'this woman doesn't want to know'. To be quite honest, I didn't care anyway.

Tom's father got the full works on my boyfriend; his hobbies, his family, how good he was at sport, how successful he was at work. He listened for a good half-hour before turning the conversation to travel, food, and sex – anything that would not relate to the boyfriend. It didn't work. But I thought Tom's father was cute, had dreamy eyes and the longest eyelashes I had ever seen. Only men have eyelashes that long and that thick. I remember thinking at the time that he would have pretty children, whoever the mother might be.

We never spoke or met again until two years later at Liverpool Street station. He was drunk. He and his friend were giving marks out of ten to the Essex commuter girls. Tom's father gave me eight and a half out of ten for my legs. He couldn't see my face: probably would have scored less if he had. When I turned round, Tom's father said, 'I know that girl'.

'No, you don't', said his friend.

'Yes, I do. She came to my birthday party two years ago. Can't remember her name but I know her.'

'No, you don't – prove it.'

'OK', he said, all macho. 'I will.'

'Hello, I know you, don't I?'

I turned round and peered at this slightly drunk, city-suited, bleary-eyed hopeful.

'No. Go away.'

'Yes, I do, you came to my birthday party at Duke's several years ago, with er ... what's her name ... Suzie ... Suzanne.'

'No, er, oh yes.' The eyelashes were coming back to me. I couldn't remember his name but it was my birthday, so what the heck. 'Oh, yes, how are you? '

'Fine, what are you doing?'

'Waiting for my boyfriend.'

'Oh.'

'We're not going out any more, but he's taking me to dinner, and I'm late and he's probably gone already but I'm waiting anyway.' (He had gone but I did wait and I did have dinner with him later that evening.)

'Oh.' He looked dejected.

'Here's my card.' I picked a card from my pocket – I always kept some to hand just in case of clinching a deal or a date. 'I'm going to Monte Carlo next week (true) to write a feature for The Independent (lie) but I will be back in a week's time (possible). Call me and we can go out for a drink or lunch or something (another possible).'

He took the card.

I was a bit adventurous in those days. My business cards were bright azure blue with such a fancy scrawl you could barely decipher what was written on them. The writing looked a bit like a spider's incomplete cobweb. Sarah Tucker looked like Silly Tinker. I received so many letters from people addressing me as Dear Ms Tinker.

****

My first date with Tom's father was at a pub down a leafy lane on the outskirts of Chelmsford. The pub is called The Duck. I dressed nicely in blouse and long flowery skirt and pumps. He wore jeans and a Gun's 'n' Roses T-shirt. Torn.

We sat and talked and I fibbed about what I had done in Monte Carlo (had a whale of a time being wined and dined and rubbing shoulders with Caroline and Stephanie and Boris Becker and Ilie

Nastase – but that's another book). Tom's father was completely open and honest and I liked him. After the affectations of Monte Carlo, he was very real and refreshing and youthful.

I got the impression that everyone is wrinkly and slightly grubby in Monte Carlo, like the money. Wrinkled because of the sun or because of their age or a combination of both. Even those who are still in their youth seem old before their time, tired by a life that offers too much money and too much time in which to waste and spend it.

Those who don't have chips in their hands have chips on their shoulders, each watching the other with suspicion. Nowhere is this general mistrust more apparent than every evening outside the Hotel de Paris, which sits adjacent to the casino. The Porsche. The Ferrari. The Aston Martin. The Lamborghini. Each glides into the square as the day turns to dusk and the craggy, the grotesque and the unspeakably beautiful slither from their gleaming, personally-plated chariots. The people are as shiny and untouchable as the cars they drive.

But back to reality; back to The Duck. All was going well with Tom's father. I was drinking lemonade, so no getting drunk and saying something I didn't mean – or worse, did mean. Then it happened. I didn't plan it. It just came up and came out. I went bright red, then silent, then giggled and relaxed. I had burped. Not a quiet little one but a definite burp, unlady-like enough to draw attention.

Tom's father told me years later that if I hadn't burped and then giggled and relaxed and started being me, instead of some wannabe, he wouldn't have wanted to see me again. I had been the Monte Carlo lady full of herself and her travels, the lemonade girl with the champagne taste. Just think, if it hadn't been for a bit of wind, Tom would not be here today.

Which leads me back to Chelmsford. Windy Chelmsford, county town of Essex; Essex – the land of the flat landscape and even flatter vowel. The people who live there, 42 minutes by train from Liverpool Street station, are split into two categories: those who commute and those who don't. Perhaps there is a sub section, of those who are married to those who commute and who behave and look somewhere between the two.

The day I left hospital, two days after giving birth to Tom, I went into town to do some Christmas shopping. It was 23 December and I had not bought any presents. I didn't have Tom with me and the sense of freedom and achievement was overwhelming. I wanted to go up to people and say 'Hi, I've just had a baby. Aren't I clever?'.

Christmas itself was a bit surreal. Everyone looked at Tom the same way they usually did the television set at Christmas: in silent awe and contemplation.

Tom woke every two hours of every day to be fed. For once in my life I had a chest, with an actual cleavage. Each morning I would wake to find the duvet wet and my nipples squirting milk into Tom's father's ear – which made me laugh and him annoyed. The first time I took Tom into town and especially to the local supermarket – men – and I presume they were fathers themselves – would come up to me and say, 'They don't stay that size for long'.

I still wonder if they were referring to Tom and not to my wondrous chest.

This comment became like a mantra and I had this reccurring premonition that my 8lb weakling would turn into a 22-pounder overnight. He did, eventually, but it took 10 months not 10 days for Tom to grow to this size.

Walking around Chelmsford, I was more aware of other mothers with their babies. The mothers looked tired which reminded me of how tired I felt. Their eyes looked dead and their babies looked unhappy. I thought to myself that if Tom was to be a happy, laid-back baby he should have a happy, laid-back mum. I explained this to Tom's father every time the inconsiderate misogynist I seemed to be living with tried to tell me that my hormones were making me more aggressive than usual.

Pre Tom, travelling had been my release, my escape and first love. It meant freedom from responsibility at home – the cooking, cleaning, ironing and, above all, the conventions of married life.

I had never rebelled as a child, in any way. I had never experimented with anything other than in the chemistry lab at school. I studied hard and did as I was told. I believed in God, that my dad was perfect and my mum was always right. But as I approached my late twenties I rebelled. If there was a system, I wanted to question it, a tradition, break it, a convention, challenge it. Travel was an escape from routine. Travelling to new places challenged me in so many different ways. Anita Roddick, the founder of Body Shop, once described travelling as a 'university without walls'. Ultimately, travel is what you make of it.

The conventional wisdom, that says new mothers should stay at home, watching television, cooking, cleaning, feeding their babies and changing their nappies, was not my idea of life. I felt I was losing all sense of self-esteem and purpose by staying put. In Chelmsford.

I remember taking Tom round the shopping precinct with me one day and getting bored within the first 10 minutes. Tom looked bored as well. That was the only time I think he ever looked bored in all his travels.

LONDON

Months One, Two and Three

For the first few weeks after Tom was born, I did stay at home, watching daytime television.

For some reason, I had always yearned to be on television myself, to present or report on the small screen or perhaps to interview famous or talented people about their lives and work. My experience to date had been limited to brief appearances on Sky News, and various appearances on daytime and morning television – in other words, nothing special. I had featured as an ad hoc travel expert on

breakfast television. The presenters would ask me where to go and I would give them ideas, telling them to book a gîte in France, or rent an apartment in Tenerife, or anything they wanted me to say which had previously been agreed and rehearsed.

Watching daytime television, though, is totally different to being a part of it. Before Tom, I had occasionally watched the morning magazine programmes when I was ill. Daytime television is light and fluffy and can be good company. However, watching the same type of programme every morning depressed me. I lost all sense of reason and confidence. I worried about characters in soap operas. Was Grant Mitchell ever going to leave EastEnders? I really cared. I wanted to bake that perfect cake. I cared about makeovers and DIY. Serious stuff, huh?

Rather than rot mentally, I decided to walk the streets of Chelmsford with Tom in his pram. I walked even when the shops were closed and there was nothing to see and nothing to do. I walked when it was raining and windy and cold. Anything was better than sitting at home watching one presenter bake a cake while another one talked about dieting. Eventually I decided to go to London.

My first trip to London was on Tom's tenth 'birth' day. He was so small and light, I put him in a front carrier. His head – about the size of a tennis ball – was completely hidden by the cover. He slept for most of the day. I took him on the Underground and on the train and even during the rush hour he didn't cause any fuss. Because he was so small I could feed him and no one knew what I was doing underneath the baby carrier.

Of course Tom had not yet received any vaccinations, because the first batch is at eight weeks. Many mums don't seem to leave the house until they believe their babies won't catch germs, so you don't see many really small newborn babies about. My doctor said fresh air would be good for Tom, and that it would help him sleep. As he was being breast-fed, he would be getting all my antibodies, anyway.

So I made these London trips with Tom often over the next few months, and we were both very happy and contented, travelling when he was so small – even though London is not the friendliest or most patient of places. I would meet friends and colleagues and occasionally go into the office of the advertising company where I had worked. I still needed to complete some work, and had meetings to arrange. I would place Tom in the middle of the boardroom table, just like a centre-piece, while I talked business. He would lie there and look up at the ceiling and coo quietly, as many newborn babies do before they discover the full range of their vocal cords.

Usually, I would change him in the toilets at stations and in shops, rather than in the designated changing rooms, which I didn't like. Often baby changing-rooms are hidden away in stores and stations as though they had 'leper' written on the door. There were no televisions or radios in these rooms, although mothers are frequently in there for quite long periods, nursing as well as changing babies.

The décor tends to be very drab too. So watching the walls was a depressing alternative and there were never any mirrors. After all, babies like to look at themselves as much as mothers do. Feeding a baby can take at least 30 minutes, and when you're new to the job, even longer. Staring at grey, dirty walls for this length of time is pretty dreary. At least in the toilet one could have privacy and kill two birds with one stone, so to speak. I don't think anyone who designs changing-rooms has ever had a baby, let alone changed one. Even in the large department stores in Oxford Street – with the exception of John Lewis, which is bright and great – I failed to find the sort of facility I expected. No wonder most mothers stay at home during the first few months.

At first, the thought of Tom picking up germs from the floor of public toilets was one of my major concerns. But I asked mothers with larger families (two or more children) their advice about changing babies in shops. These mums were much calmer about the whole process than those who had just given birth to their first child, like me. They told me that they had been ultra-careful with their first babies, but by the second, third, or fourth, had gradually become more practical and realistic about what they could and couldn't do with their children while travelling in town. They gave me common-sense, no-nonsense advice. Yes, it is important to have nappies and baby milk and toys at the ready, but you don't need to carry a suitcase for your journey.

One woman I spoke to carried only a nappy and a nappy sack in her pocket, and that was it. 'When you travel, babies are surrounded by potential toys as well as by potential hazards. Anyone who has handled a baby will know door keys, car keys, any sort of keys are much more interesting than soft toys.'

As Tom grew and I took him to town more regularly, I quickly came to the conclusion that Londoners don't like babies very much.

Looking back, I found London to be by far the most unfriendly place for a mother to travel with a young baby. In Paris, in Stockholm, in Toronto, even in Bangkok and Sydney, people were friendly, helpful and considerate, certainly to this mother and her baby.

For example, take the London Underground. Or rather, don't take the London Underground. OK, so it's under reconstruction. It's been under reconstruction for the past decade. But are they 'reconstructing' more lifts for mothers with babies? Not to my knowledge. And the number of escalators still doesn't seem to improve even when the stations have undergone reconstruction. There are too many stairs and not enough escalators.

If you are able bodied and without a baby, the Underground is almost bearable outside the rush hour, but it is still dirty, unhygienic and overcrowded. If you have a baby with you, it can be dangerous. You and your baby are an inconvenience which other travellers tolerate at best, push about at worst. On stairs, people would push me from behind in the full knowledge that I had a baby in a front carrier. I would turn round and apologise for being there and they would perhaps feel guilty for pushing. And I would then feel guilty for making them feel guilty.

Compare that with my experience in Paris. The Metro was just as crowded, if not more so, but the Parisians would give up their seats without being asked. They would open doors for you and generally give you the space and time you needed as a mum travelling with a baby. In fact, I saw many mothers with newborn babies on the Paris Metro. I probably only noticed them as I was in the same situation myself.

I have recently been told by the London Tourist Board that there have been many recent improvements to London Transport for parents with children in pushchairs. It is true that the DLR and new Jubilee line stations are all accessible, and many low floor buses run on routes throughout London. Of course, if you can afford it, go by taxi. You will almost certainly find the London cabbie friendly and helpful with buggies and luggage.

****

Overground trains (the privatised service formerly known as British Rail) are as inconsistent in their service to mothers with babies as they are in their punctuality. Some services offer much better facilities than others: in my experience Virgin and Eurostar are amongst the best.

One journey I took with Tom in his front carrier (to interview the MD of a company called Baby Organix, Lizzie Vann), meant that I had to travel from Chelmsford in Essex to Christchurch in Dorset, a journey of some hours. I was due to interview Lizzie about the organic baby food her company produced and I thought it would be a good idea to take Tom along.

Tom had already travelled to London many times by week eight, and the additional part of the journey – a train ride from Waterloo to Christchurch – would be just an additional jaunt for him. He liked the movement of the train, the sound and the motion. He must have grown accustomed to it while I was pregnant as I commuted to and from Chelmsford to Liverpool Street. The journey usually sent him to sleep while he was inside me, and it seemed to have the same effect after he was born.

Lizzie Vann was wonderful, a breath of fresh air after a very long and very hot and stuffy journey. We met in a small boardroom surrounded by displays of all her baby food products. She told me that airlines presently failed to offer organic baby food, and that only a few offered baby food at all. She was really inspirational when I told her that I wanted to travel to other countries with Tom. She said she would let me know where to find organic baby food in all the countries I intended to visit with my son.

Tom was brilliant, sleeping or cooing for most of the time. Smelly nappy but happy chap. On the way home, I changed him on a toilet cubicle floor at Waterloo. It looked relatively clean and I placed him on the inside of my blazer while I did my 30-second wash and wipe trick. Tom was unimpressed by my expertise and dexterity.

Two weeks later I received a large box from Lizzie, full of organic food for Tom, to be eaten when he had reached four and seven months. Lizzie's range, especially the desserts, tastes good enough for grown ups. In fact, I don't think Tom's eaten a single dessert – they all taste so good. Every time I buy a pot at the supermarket, I eat it myself. They are full of ingredients like figs and sultanas and apricots and they make a wonderful healthy snack. And anyway, Tom's nappies are smelly enough already, thank you.

Our trip to Dorset fuelled us both for our next journey: over the sea, to Ireland.

IRELAND

Three Months

Tom is a plastic paddy. His father is a plastic paddy, an O'Reilly although he was born in Derby. So Tom is Thomas O'Reilly, an Irish name if ever there was one.

OK. So my maiden name is Tucker. I use it in my work because Sarah Tucker sounds good. It's a strong name and I think my dad would have been pleased that I kept it. But Tucker is not Tom's name. (Although Tommy Tucker does have a certain ring to it – don't you think?)

I therefore thought Ireland should be one of the countries he should visit first. It seemed one of the easiest places to go: they speak English in most parts, the weather is rarely sunny and hot – which Tom doesn't particularly like – and the Irish like babies. Well, that is a bit of an understatement. Let's just say, they have the same enthusiasm for babies that the Brazilians have for football. They run the Italians close in their love for babies, but whereas the Italians I later discovered are tactile and prone to picking babies up at the slightest opportunity, in Ireland they choose to sing to them as well. And boy, can the Irish sing lullabies.

****

We flew from Stansted, which is about half an hour's drive from where I live. The airport building is modern and clean and welcoming.

It looks like a giant greenhouse, but – unlike a greenhouse – it is wonderfully cool inside. Thankfully, although BA's younger sister Go now flies from there, I have never witnessed crowds at Stansted, with or without Tom.

The first challenge is to manoeuvre your way through the swing doors at the entrance. If you have a push chair, any swing door is a potential weapon as far as your baby is concerned. Trapped hands, trapped heads, trapped feet. Many a nightmare I had in the first few

months of my journeys with Tom at airports, which involved him nearly losing a limb in one of these contraptions. Swing doors and lifts: lethal.

When we went to Ireland, Tom travelled in the front carrier. He was still light enough and I wanted him close to me. He was starting to be more aware of his surroundings and rather than turning him to face me and my milk-heavy boobs, I placed him facing outwards. The bright lights in the terminal fascinated him.

There were plenty of sofas to lounge around on, and shops to spend money in. I resisted the temptation to buy soft toys although Tom had already developed antennae for them and reached out to each fluffy face as we passed by the aisles.

The ladies' toilet did not have a changing facility, but it was clean and large and empty when I went in with Tom. I was now an expert at balancing him on my knee to change his nappy, whipping off the old and on the new.

Boarding the plane was made easier by having Tom with me. I remember in my travels as a journalist having to wait until 'mothers with young children' and 'those who require assistance on to the plane' had boarded first. Now I thought hey, I'm one of them. Tom was a passport to first class treatment even if I wasn't in a first class seat.

The seat. Ah yes. If you can get an upgrade to business class, go for it. The extra space really helps. There is just enough space for one adult in standard class seats on most flights. So with a young baby nestled against your bosom, you are sardine-like squashed.

I had notified Aer Lingus in advance that Tom would be travelling with me and asked if they could give me a seat with more space. I got an aisle seat near the front of the plane which gave me more leg-room and Tom room to breathe. Otherwise Tom could well have spent the journey with his nose pressed up against the in-flight magazine and the sick bag. I would also be able to pop to the toilets if Tom needed changing without continually disturbing the person next to me.

The plane was full. Luckily I had just fed Tom so he was sleepy, because I had two hours in which to keep him occupied and quiet. There would be a lot to see on the plane without the need for toys, soft or otherwise.

An elderly lady sat next to me. Not the sweet old lady you see in old black and white films, just an old lady who looked utterly cross about being old and sitting next to someone who wasn't who had a baby on her lap. Perhaps Tom would puke all over her. He didn't. He was wonderful. He stared at everyone with his big blue eyes and grinned. He grinned at the airline hostess, who took him off to be introduced to the captain, which I thought was a bit risky. After all, Tom might have mistaken an on/off switch for a play thing.

Tom was also manhandled by a few of my fellow passengers (most of whom were Irish) with the exception, of course, of the old lady next to me. He had a thoroughly good time, in fact so good that he fell asleep for the last hour of the journey. And I did too.

****

Another reason for making this trip to Ireland was that I wanted to retrace my first journey five years earlier to Dublin and to the west coast of southern Ireland. I had travelled with Tom's father to Dublin, to meet his friends. On that journey, we had hired a car in Dublin and driven to the west coast, to the town of Newport and then on to Dingle.

The friends in Dublin had four children, all under the age of five. At the time I decided I definitely did not want children. Although all were extremely well behaved, utterly gorgeous and loveable, when we travelled with them they dictated where and when we ate, the places and pace at which we walked, the shops we did and didn't enter. Everything we did that day was geared towards them – though they never needed to say 'I want'.

When they were in bed, having been bathed and kissed and read and sung to, we went to a trendy restaurant in the heart of Dublin. The Lord of the Dance, Michael Flatley himself, was there with a pretty companion. And no, I didn't ask for an interview. I would have done, but I had left my tape recorder at home.

Newport in County Mayo is a charming little town on Clew Bay. We stayed at a lovely country house hotel – Newport House – for a few nights before heading south, down the coast towards Dingle.

Newport House allowed guests the option of fishing for their own supper. But Tom's father decided to give the angling a miss and we chose from a selection caught earlier by a professional: we ate it grilled – plain and simple and delicious.

The owner of the hotel was extraordinarily friendly, even by Irish standards. Her manner was extremely courteous as she greeted all visitors.

'Welcome, welcome to Newport House. So nice of you to come. So nice. It's lovely to meet you. Really quite wonderful. You are … ?'

This technique became a talking point among the guests. The owner was always there to greet you, as if appearing by magic – like Mr Benn's shopkeeper – itching to please. It got to the point where I expected her to jump out of the wardrobe each morning with a bathrobe, or spring from under the bed with a tray of freshly brewed tea and hot-from-the-oven soda bread and local butter and home-made jam. It was a bit unnerving really.

One day, we found a little restaurant overlooking the river estuary, where we ate fresh oysters and mussels in the hope that the aphrodisiac effect would sweep us away. It didn't. I suffered a bad reaction to a mussel and went as red as a tomato, got hot and sweaty and tingly all over. (Bit like sex really, but without the pleasure: not quite what we had in mind.)

Next we travelled to Dingle. The town is well named. Dingle is as Dingle sounds: eccentric, quaint, full of New Age drifters. It is charming, full of character and characters.

As a result, Dingle has become a place visitors go to find their 'inner selves', to find themselves spiritually. Ironically the first time we visited Dingle, we found we were lost. Physically not spiritually, that is.

There was a pub opposite the small bed-and-breakfast that we booked into for the night. The local musicians sang and played guitar every afternoon and evening in the pub. Everyone drank Guinness and sang in perfect harmony to songs nothing to do with Abba, The Beatles or Simon and Garfunkel. You don't find punters singing in pubs in England unless they are completely drunk. And when they do sing, it's usually a rugby or football anthem.

****

It was to this land of enthusiasm, warmth, friendliness and delightful pub singing that I brought my son when he was only three months old. At this age, Thomas looked like an angel and the Irish treated him as one. He also had the added value of an Irish name, O'Reilly, as I have explained.

Dublin Airport was busy when Tom and I arrived. Not that there was any sense of anyone being in a hurry to get anywhere. Everyone obviously had to get somewhere but without a deadline. I had only one suitcase with me, plus a large bag containing Tom's clothes, nappies and favourite toy.

Tom loved the airport. It was love at first sight, really. Stansted had been a bit quiet, like a very large, very well lit waiting room, which is really what an airport is on a grand scale. At Stansted, everyone waited patiently, said very little, just shopped and ate and drank quietly.

The airport at Dublin was a totally different proposition. The Irish are not a nation to speak quietly or move quietly, or to be quiet for that matter. In the south the soft lilt of their voices resembles a lullaby. But it is a loud lullaby, and I'm sure that any after-dinner speaker would envy their natural voice projection. There was a lot of noise in the airport in Dublin that day.

Car hire. Where was it? Trolleys, where were they? I couldn't find either. Fortunately I had invested in one of those cases with wheels and a long handle, so I was able to walk along with Tom round my waist looking at the world, the bag over my shoulder and the case trailing behind me somewhere. Dare I say, I felt almost in control.

I found car hire. A man with a lullaby voice and dark blue Irish eyes cooed at Tom from behind the counter. Tom cooed back.

'Ah, and who is this little one. Boy or girl?'

'Boy. Tom O'Reilly.'

I wanted to try out the Irish sympathy vote from the word go. It worked.

'Ah, an Irish laddie then. Well now, isn't he just beautiful. How old?'

'Three months.'

'Three months, eh? He's a big boy for three months. I have five of my own. Very happy I am too. How many do you have?'

'This is my first.'

'But you want more, yes?'

'Well, I don't know. See how I cope with this one.'

'Oh, you will want more. Only children are a bit strange you know. Emotional cripples. Bit full of their own importance. Think they can do anything. No one to play with. They can't share. Must have more than one, my dear.'

'I'm an only child', I said.

End of conversation.

I hired a Golf GTi, something nippy and fast and easy to park. It was dark green and in good condition. I had also pre-ordered a car seat for Tom, fixed beside me to the front passenger seat so that he could see me and I could see him. He was enjoying himself. I remember thinking 'this is much more exciting than staying at home watching television'. I'm sure he was thinking the same thing.

The roads were easy to negotiate, although the drivers in Dublin reminded me of those in Rome: chaotic. You needed to have your wits about you all the time. I was even more aware of potential hazards having Tom with me.

Some baby experts recommend putting babies in the back seat of the car, rather than the front, partly for safety reasons and partly so that they don't distract the driver. But I liked Tom in the front. At traffic lights I would sit and wait patiently and smile at him and he would smile back at me. Pre-Tom, I sat at traffic lights, tutting and cursing, showing the first symptoms of impending road rage if red failed to turn to green within ten seconds of stopping. Tom made me a calmer and more considerate driver, if not a slower one.

I headed straight for Newport and the famous welcome. I wondered how the lady of the house would react to Tom. If she gave me any funny comments about Tom being an only child, I would stay somewhere else.

I needn't have worried. She hugged me. She hugged Tom and sang to him. But he was tired and needed feeding, so started to cry. I told her not to take it personally, but people always do when babies cry exclusively in their arms. She looked mortified.

Newport House had a lot to entertain children and good facilities for babies. There was a baby-minding facility that I hadn't noticed on my previous visit. And that's what I liked about the hotel. It didn't look purpose-built for families so that courting couples felt out of place, nor the other way round. Everyone seemed to mix naturally.

Nothing was too much trouble. A cot was provided in the room. There was a baby listening service free of charge, and if you wanted one a babysitter on call, for a minimal charge. The hotel provided baby food – organic and non-genetically modified. The beds were as I remembered: large and four poster, with Egyptian cotton sheets and all-enveloping duvets.

Tom slept better in Ireland than in any other country on our travels. Perhaps it was the Irish air, or the fact that people would continually sing to him, or the fact that when they spoke it sounded like a lullaby anyway – their lilting voices were so melodic and tuneful. The fact they also spoke nineteen to the dozen may have been quite tiring to listen to. Even if he could have answered back, I doubt if he would have got a word in edgeways.

After a few days in Newport House, we bid a tearful farewell. By now, Tom had produced the right quota of smiles and cooing to make the owner happy. Dingle beckoned.

When I visited Dingle before, we stayed in a small bed and breakfast in the centre of town, opposite a rather noisy pub. The pub culture wasn't one I wanted to introduce Tom to at this stage as the atmosphere was smoky. This was a great pity as the pub culture in Ireland is quite unique and to my mind an essential part of the Irish experience. The Irish sing and talk about life, love and everything in the pub as they drink their Guinness – which everyone always tells me tastes better in Ireland than it does in England. But I didn't want to subject Tom to smoke. The Irish may not be as heavy smokers as the French or Italians or Spanish, but they are closing the gap.

The restaurants and cafes are a different matter. Most of them have no smoking areas which is helpful if you have a young baby. They are also very accommodating and knowledgeable about how to treat babies in even the most select restaurant. They prepare a table which allows you ample space for the buggy out of the way of both the waiters and other customers. This seems only common sense, but when I travelled in England, such foresight was sadly lacking in all the restaurants I visited.

The famous Myrtle Allen cookery school at Ballymaloe, just outside Shanagarry, is a good example of how babies are an important issue in Ireland. Myrtle's daughter-in-law Darina, who now runs the school, offers cookery courses on preparing healthy and interesting food for children, and the children who visit are the testers. They are treated with the same amount of respect as their parents. The cots provided look as comfortable as the beds for the adults. If you need to interrupt your meal after the first course to look after your baby and then return an hour later, no problem. If you want to play croquet between the second and third course, no problem. Ballymaloe provided a good example of how relaxed the Irish are with babies and children. I received nothing but sensible advice, and then only when I asked for it. The restaurants and hotels are friendly to families without compromising the charms for the adults. There is no question of being confined to highly coloured, purpose-built, 'child friendly' places to stay or to eat. The Irish trip was a holiday for me as much as it was for Tom. And there are not many places I could say that about.

LESSONS LEARNT IN IRELAND

1. Baby Watch
Be aware of what your baby can see and what stimulates him while travelling. Facing into you he can only see and sense you. Facing out – once he is strong enough to hold his head up – he can still sense you, and know that you are there to protect him, but he sees much more around him.

2. Quick change
Learn and practise until you are adept at changing your baby quickly given limited space. If there are no changing facilities available at airports, in shops, or at least ones you are happy with, all you need is a disposable changing mat (Pampers do good ones) and a toilet floor, plus dexterity.

3. Mothers with children first
Boarding planes is made easier with a baby or child – you should be allowed on first to 'get yourself settled'. Some airlines leave more time than others before they allow the other passengers on. Virgin, BA, Emirates, Air New Zealand and Air Canada allowed the most time on my travels. For shorter haul carriers, it's starter's orders I'm afraid.

4. Babies and upgrades
Most of us can't afford business or first-class tickets, so the only chance of more space is an upgrade. In my experience it is far less likely you will be offered an upgrade if you have a baby in tow, as the baby will probably disturb the other passengers. Those airlines I asked about possible upgrades (even if you are a journalist with a baby) said that there is no official policy of discriminating for or against passengers who seek upgrades who also have babies. Each airline is individual. If you don't ask, you don't get. Just like a normal upgrade, if you are a journalist, on honeymoon, or you are a seasoned traveller with a particular airline already, it will help. In addition, looking smart and having a silent, smiling baby is a bonus.

5. Think strategic
Think strategically when asking for seats on planes for both long and short haul. Choose one close to the toilet (for efficiency of changing) and an aisle seat near the front which allows more space for you and your baby. For most long haul flights a variety of cots will be offered (which you must ask for when you book your flight). This will automatically give you a seat which has more space for the cot and you.

6. Think minimalist

Think minimalist when packing: always consider that you need your hands free. Anything which means you can keep at least one hand around the front carrier containing your baby will make life easier. Wherever you are going, regardless of for how long and how far, keep it down to one suitcase with wheels. You can do it.

7. Car seats overseas

When driving hire cars, you do need a proper car seat if you have a baby with you. All major car hire companies provide one for a fee. Just tell them what type you need and also how much your baby weighs. If you want to take your own, make sure it fits into the model of car the company offers: some car seats don't fit some cars. Also, if you decide to take your own car seat on the flight, don't forget that you will have the added hassle of an un-carry-item to lug through airport security at the other end of the flight. It will probably be too unwieldy to check in with the rest of your luggage, so you will either have to check it in at the 'special counter' (long queues) or carry it until you get to the plane itself, when an air hostess will take it from you. Unnecessary hassle.

8. 'Family friendly' hotels and restaurants

Just because hotels and restaurants don't actually publicise the fact that they cater for babies and children, doesn't always mean they don't. Choose the hotels and restaurants you want to go to – and then enquire if they have facilities for mothers with babies. You may be pleasantly surprised. It is limiting to pick just those outlets and hotels which overtly cater for 'families', which, in my experience, usually means everything will be distinctly un-grown-up.

9. Manage expectations

Manage the expectations of the restaurants and hotels you are visiting. Tell them how old your baby is, if he can sit up, if you need space for a cot or high chair, and that you may need to breast- or bottle-feed. Is this acceptable? If you explain everything before you arrive, they will be better prepared and will make your stay more enjoyable. Most places will adapt to your needs if they can, but not in every country.

FRANCE

Three Months

I have wonderful childhood memories of France. My parents would take me to the south of France each summer. My mother worked part-time and my father, as a deputy head, always had the benefit of long school holidays, so we had six weeks of glorious sunshine and French accents.

We crossed the Channel by hovercraft as it was quicker and easier than taking a ferry. Then from Calais the Tucker family headed straight for signs saying *autoroute à péage*.

My parents never discovered the delights of the D roads and the wonderful little towns and villages you discover along the way if you have more time and patience. We would (as my father would say) 'belt' down the autoroute from Calais to Nice, in a day and a bit, stopping only for the occasional Marks & Spencer picnic which – in Blue Peter style – my mother had made earlier.

I remember as a child watching the road signs and counting down the kilometres until we hit Paris. I then drew or daydreamed until we reached the sign for Chalon *nord* and Chalon *sud*, then fall asleep and wake up at Macon *nord* and Macon *sud*. Then I might read a book until Lyon *nord* and Lyon *sud*, start to get irritable at Avignon *nord* and Avignon *sud* before we eventually reached Nice. Which had no *nord* or *sud* according to the signs.

I used to dread the Paris *périphérique*, as my mum would always start to yell at my dad:

'You're in the wrong lane, Norman. Move over. You're in the wrong lane. Move over. Move over now!' in her best Hyacinth Bucket voice.

The black plastic of the car seat would get hotter and stickier as we drove southward, and the journey more uncomfortable. A Ford Cortina E had no air conditioning in those days. One escape from the increasingly uncomfortable journey was to look out of the window and watch the surrounding countryside. The fields would change from deep olive green to sun-bleached yellow, and the roofs of the houses and barns from dull grey to warm ochre.

Occasionally we would stop for my father to have some sleep or a cup of coffee. He did all the driving, as my mum hadn't yet passed her test. Strange that. From the way she told my father how to drive, you would think she had. My dad needed the extra strong, teeny-weeny cups of coffee, which the French make so well, even in motorway cafés. By the time we hit the last straight my father would be buzzing with caffeine.

We camped in France. The Tuckers would never stay in a hotel: too expensive for six weeks on a teacher's salary. The only time we didn't camp was when we went with my aunt and uncle one year. That year we stayed in a luxury self-catering apartment in Juan les Pins. The apartment had a communal swimming pool. I remember it distinctly because this was where I learnt to dive.

I actually preferred staying under canvas. We would arrive tired and hot and sweaty at an oasis of plane and pine trees and be led by a smiling Frenchman to the designated rectangle of land where we could pitch our tent. Each rectangle had a tree, which would be our shade for the next six weeks. If you were lucky, it was well developed and gave good shade. If you were unlucky, it was a sapling. We had saplings some years.

Some French families, resident in their rectangle the whole summer, made this space their second home. They even grew tomatoes and beans. Presumably French beans.

The sun would shine relentlessly for six weeks, until the rains and the mistral came in late August. We would then have torrential rain for several days, during which the ditches we dug around our tent at the beginning of our stay would save us from being flooded.

A camping holiday was a good way to make friends. Being an only child, I had no brothers or sisters to play with, chat to or hide behind.

I would ask my parents for a bag of sweets or crisps and use this device as a means to get other children to talk to me. 'Hello, my name is Sarah. Would you like a crisp?' I even learnt to say this in French. Most of the time the tactic worked, and saved me from swimming in circles by myself in the pool or talking to imaginary friends.

I would race into the nearby forests and collect pine cones with my new friends, Maria or Marcel. We would swap toys. I would always swap badly. At the end of the holiday we would exchange addresses and hugs and cry, and promise to write to each other forever. We never did.

My parents gave me a few simple chores to do each day. I collected the bread, the milk and the ice for the ice box (a DIY freezer cabinet for campers) each morning. By the age of four I was already well versed in how to order the provisions in the campsite shop. I collected the baguettes, croissants and *lait et crème*. I would then return with a bucket or bowl, into which a man would slice a chunk of ice for the icebox with a large pick.

What vivid and strange memories one has as a child. I loved France. Still do. Perhaps that's why I decided to make it the next place I would visit with Tom. That, and the fact that the French are supposed to like children. I wanted to find this out for myself.

****

In order to leave England, Tom obviously had to have a passport. I had left it a bit late to arrange this. The law had changed the year before so babies had to have their own passports. Before that, they could share their parents'. A 'baby passport' lasted five years, and although it seemed ridiculous that a five-year-old would have a passport with a picture of him or her at the age of five months, in principle it seemed a good idea.

The main problem with a baby passport is the photo. You need a picture of the baby without you holding it. If you have a three month old, he can't sit up by himself so you have to hold him up. I have yet to see a photo booth which takes photos from the ceiling. Most people resort to putting their baby on a white sheet on a bed and straddling above them, shoot from on high. Then the picture has to be reproduced twice, which is a requirement of the passport office, and cut to 'passport size'.

One day while shopping, I went into the local Boots and took Tom to the photo booth.

I went in and sat down on the stool and read the instructions.

'Put the money in the slot.' Done.

'Position your head in the red circle you see in front of you.' In this case I put Tom's head in the red circle. He looked bemused. I looked flustered. I was in the picture. I covered my head with Tom's white crochet blanket, just being able to see that he was still in the red circle. Sort of.

I clasped him with my arm just below his tummy to keep him upright. My arm looked like his leg. It looked as though he had contorted his leg into a very strange position over his right shoulder. Well, babies are supposed to be supple, I thought.

Click.

Light flash.

One picture taken. Do I like it? You have ten seconds to decide.

Tom looked constipated in the image on the screen in front of us. I thought we would give it another go. 'Press button to start again.' I pressed button to start again. Tom was starting to enjoy this game. A smile, even.

Click.

Flash of light. Another picture taken. Better. Tom looked less constipated. Surprised definitely, but at least not constipated. It would do. Two minutes later, £2.50 poorer, I had four painless passport photos. Next, I went to the post office. A form to complete. Also I needed a witness, a professional, someone who could vouch for Tom being Tom. I went to our solicitor who quite rightly insisted on seeing Tom. Thankfully she agreed that there was a resemblance between my son and me. 'You can never be too careful', she said. Yeah, right.

I sweet-talked the man behind the post office counter into putting extra specially urgent on the envelope and, after much cooing from Tom who was starting to enjoy the whole experience, I left the post office in the hope of seeing a bright red passport arrive in a week's time.

It did. Just in time. And Tom still looked constipated.

****

Now three months old, Tom was already absorbing everything around him. He was alert to the new smells, the new light, the new voices, the colours, and the new warmth in the air. He seemed mesmerised by the whole experience of travel.

I took Tom to France by ferry. The particular route I chose was from Portsmouth to St Malo. I don't like Portsmouth, but I do like St Malo. It is a pretty port, small and unspoilt by the ferry-loads of tourists in their cars and on foot.

We travelled by car, on a night crossing. I booked a standard cabin.

Don't go by car, on a night crossing, and book a standard cabin, if you have a baby.

For a start, the journey begins at about 8 o'clock in the evening, which is Tom's bed-time. But there is far too much going on for anyone to sleep, let alone a baby. A standard cabin, though clean and highly functional if there is one adult, or even two, has limited dimensions, and if you have – as I do – one of those travel cots which doubles as a playpen, it takes up the floor space. Not some of the floor space. All of the floor space.

I recommend you to book a luxury cabin. It is worth every penny.

Next, announcements. On ships there are announcements all the time. Sometimes these are about the ship leaving, sometimes about the opening and closing and serving times in the restaurant, or the film about to start or the latest perfume on offer. These announcements are always boomed out in each cabin. The cut off time is usually around 10 pm, and they start up again at 5 in the morning. Hence it is possible to get an early morning wake-up call of Chanel Number Five, offering a free photo frame if you care to rush to the ship shop sharp. Charming.

Feeding myself and Tom proved easier. Brittany Ferries serve a variety of baby food on their ships, whilst the food for adults is good.

As a new mother in England I was weary of compromising for Tom when it came to eating out. I always ate bland food in gaudy restaurants so that Tom could eat in a baby friendly environment. Notable exceptions in London and Chelmsford are Pizza Express, Café Rouge and Café Uno. But you can only eat so many *salades niçoises*.

Back on the ferry, no one blinked an eyelid as I nursed Tom under my shirt in the restaurant, as I attempted to tuck into, well, a *salade niçoise*. Our ferry was geared for families with children. There was a play area, a cinema (but no films showing) and high chairs available in all the restaurants. I hadn't asked for a cot, but I believe you could have one if you booked it in advance. Everyone was friendly and helpful.

The seas were relatively calm and the gentle rocking and rolling of the ship seemed to help Tom sleep more deeply. So much so, that when we got our early-morning-Chanel Number 5-with-free-photo-frame-wake-up-call, he was most disgruntled.

Tom likes cars. It's not just a male thing, it's a baby thing. Most parents will tell you tales of driving around in the night with their own little Tommy in the back seat when they can't get him to sleep in his cot.

It's the motion, and the warmth, and perhaps the closeness of the baby seat that makes a child doze off. Anyway, it works, and it made travelling with Tom through France very easy.

Rather than venture down the *autoroute à péage* on my first journey, I headed for Brittany and the Loire via the D routes my parents avoided.

I had booked our little family into a self-catering apartment in the upmarket seaside resort of La Baule just south of the Brittany coast.

The weather was mixed: in fact, it rained a lot. It's supposed to rain a lot in Brittany, but I wanted sunshine. I hadn't been able to acquire a tan since giving birth to Tom and I was looking positively pasty. Normally, I am a devout sun worshipper, but because you should try to keep a baby in the shade all the time, the mother usually has to do the same. On our trips out I would contort my body on park benches to get a shin or an elbow into some warm rays while the rest of me stayed in the shade with Tom.

The apartment was clean and central and the neighbours were friendly but nosey. They loved Tom. As I walked out of the front door each morning I would see the net curtains of the neighbouring houses start to twitch. Suddenly, there would be Madame St Pierre with her poodle, talking in broken English to me, and utter gibberish to Tom. The French, or at least the French who live in La Baule, are a tactile lot. They loved holding Tom. They seemed to sense when and how a baby wanted to be picked up and talked to and played with. They did it without hesitation, instinctively, and usually (although they occasionally forgot in their excitement) asked my permission.

Not only did they talk and coo and play with Tom, they also wanted to introduce him to the rest of their families. They passed him round like a parcel, each saying exactly the same thing to him, careless of the fact that he didn't understand a word. He smiled at them.

To be fair, Tom didn't understand a word of what I was saying either, so in a way baby gibberish became a universal language, which we could all relate to: a bit like music, really.

Tom and I were even welcomed in posh frock shops. There were a lot of posh frock shops in La Baule. Many wealthy Parisians had second homes in the town, and the local retailers catered for a market which had the money but not the time to spend it.

Everyone looked immaculate and stylish, even when they had a baby in tow. They would wheel their babies in immaculate little pushchairs, pushchairs with matching colours and frills. The baby's outfit would compliment the colours and frills of the pushchair and also match the mother's outfit, which would match the poodle's outfit.

Ordinarily, without Tom, this co-ordinated clique of ladies-who-lunch would have ignored the rather ill-kempt English tourist walking along the street. But with Tom, despite the fact that my clothes, his clothes and the colours on the front carrier clashed horribly, there was always a smile, a *bonjour*, and a stop for a chat.

To avoid sticky fingers on the finest silk and linen outfits, the posh frock shop owners would insist on holding and playing with Tom while I searched through the racks for the elusive best buy.

'Ah, but Madame, you must buy something for the little one. Something matching perhaps?'

Perhaps not. At £50 for a baby designer T-shirt, Tom would have to be happy with his Baby Bloggs matching culottes and jumper for £15.

Restaurants in La Baule entered a whole new dimension of helpfulness. The staff made room for the pushchair, even asking people to move their tables a little, to ensure that Tom could at least see me while I tucked into my steak frîtes. The restaurants were bustling and noisy, and Tom didn't need his toys with all the activity surrounding him. He had amusement enough watching the reed-slim waiters pass to and fro, with trays of food and bottles of something light and fruity or rich and buttery.

It was pure theatre. Tom's fascination with everything made me more aware and alert to my environment. He allowed me to appreciate the detail of my surroundings. I had always felt that, as a journalist, I was a trained and practised observer, but Tom noticed things I missed. To him, everything was special. The black and white starched outfits of the staff; the tiny monograms on the cuffs and collars. The way the steam from the coffee swirled in the air as it was poured into the cup. The grace of the waiter, who like a magician, mixed and matched the ingredients for steak tartare at a neighbouring table.

Tom didn't like the sun much, though. He didn't mind the heat, which made him drowsy and thirsty, but he didn't like the bright light in his eyes and on his skin.

As well as posh frock shops, La Baule was also well stocked with supermarkets. One fact parents forget when they travel is that 'foreigners' have babies too. And yes, they do use nappies, and yes, their babies do eat baby food. You can even buy organic baby food, which hasn't been genetically modified. I found the people serving in the supermarkets helpful as to what size nappy I should choose for Tom. If I couldn't tell by the packaging, I would dangle Tom in front of the shop assistant, who would glance at his bottom and point at the relevant pack. Simple.

After a week of self catering in La Baule I decided to try a bit of luxury. A five star hotel on the edge of the Loire, just outside the town of Saumur, to be precise. Formerly a sixteenth century priory with a turret and wonderful views, the hotel had a restaurant serving the local produce, fresh that day, at a fraction of the price you would pay in England.

We were escorted to a room with an en suite bathroom. Until then, I had always bathed Tom in a baby bath but had not taken it to France – too cumbersome. So, when I bathed, Tom went in with me. He loved it. Most bathrooms are extremely well lit, and Tom loved the bright lights and the feeling of being close to me.

I wanted to eat and drink in private that night, and the hotel supplied a baby monitoring service. Very thorough. They informed me when Tom was crying, cooing, laughing – basically of anything and everything he did, other than sleep. After an hour of being told his every movement, I asked that unless he started to cough up blood, I was to be kept blissfully ignorant of his every burble.

Looking out over the Loire on that warm evening in May, I knew I would take Tom back to the Priory when he was older. I would dine with him, when he would be old enough to indulge in a little foie gras and something special from the local cellar, and I would be older, more wrinkled and hopefully a little wiser.

Our last week in France was spent in the middle of a vineyard.

I had researched tour companies who catered for families with young babies, and one of the best was a company called Gîtes de France. In their brochure, they advise how close you are to the local supermarket, to the nearest town, and doctor and dentist. Gîtes with cots and nannies on call are also mentioned. In fact, you are told everything you need to know if you have a baby, newborn or otherwise. My gîte was La Folière, owned by M. Guillet, just outside a village called Corcoue sur Logne, just west of Nantes.

It was charming and simple. It had three bedrooms, with a cot and even a baby bath supplied, and a changing mat. Toys and bunk bed were all on site. Someone had even kindly left an unopened pack of nappies and baby wipes.

The view was wonderful. We were completely surrounded by vineyards. M. Guillet introduced me to his wines and told me all about the grapes and when they were harvested. He explained what a good year it had been and asked if I would like to buy a few cases.

Yes, I would. And I did.

The gîte had a small patio and garden, in which a resident donkey grazed. The donkey, whose name was Frederick, was born the same year as me. Apparently, in the past, Fred was ridden by the children of visiting families and would happily clip-clop along all day but now he was far too old. He seemed happy just to stand and sleep, or be fed with the brioches and croissants I gave him each morning. Tom was unfazed by Fred. He smelt funny and didn't do much. In fact, the flies which surrounded Fred's mane were much more interesting. They were more active and at least they made a buzzing sound.

The Guillet family would look after Tom while I visited the nearby foie gras factories and bought pots of the local duck liver pâté. They even tried to teach him French, to say *bonjour* and *merci*. Perhaps it worked. Sometimes I'm sure I can hear him say ''allo, 'allo'.

LESSONS LEARNT IN FRANCE

1. Cross channel choice – speed is of the essence

You can only keep a baby amused for so long – even one that is very young. Consider this carefully when choosing between a ferry crossing, hovercraft, the Eurostar/Eurotunnel Shuttle or flying across the English Channel. In my experience, speed is of the essence and I found the easiest way to do this journey was usually the quickest – regardless of the baby care facilities available during the journey. If you don't have a car, take the Eurostar and let the train take the strain. It's efficient, quick and clean. If you do have a car, go by Shuttle. If you want to fly, there are more and more really cheap flights between London and Paris – and the airlines that cater for the discount market (Buzz, Go etc) are OK with babies and mothers. But if you are flying to Paris Charles de Gaulle airport isn't particularly mother and baby friendly in my experience.

2. Universal language

You will quickly discover when you travel that 'baby talk' is a universal language. Everyone will understand your baby's babblings if they have one of their own. Go into a supermarket and if you need nappies, baby food, creams and lotions, they will understand as you have a living and breathing 'prop' in the form of your baby on which to demonstrate your requirements.

3. They have babies overseas too

Don't overload yourself with nappies and toys. They take up valuable space and you need to keep luggage minimal. Nappies are either cheaper or the same price in all the places I have visited overseas. You don't need many toys unless your baby has already developed a craving for one particular comfort toy. He will be surrounded by enough attention and stimuli to keep him going for years.

4. On the road

Perhaps I just struck lucky, but the roadside stops on French autoroutes catered brilliantly for mothers with babies. Baby-changing facilities were clean, spacious (they even had toddler toilets), with disposable nappy machines, nappy sack machines, cotton wool machines. Brilliant. The larger garages, with shops attached, even sold baby food.

ITALY

Four Months

After the delights of the vineyard in France, rather than head for the South I decided to change countries altogether.

France and Italy have always been, and probably always will be my favourite countries in Europe. Perhaps it is because my parents took me so frequently to these two countries as a child that I wanted to return to both of them at the beginning of my travels with Tom. Perhaps it was also because I knew Italians are even more enamoured of *bambinos* than the French are of *bébés*.

We continued our journey south by car, pausing but briefly at Avignon, skirting round Monte Carlo – where a baby is merely another designer accessory – and then headed for Menton, further along the coast.

My aim was to return to Lucca, a place I had visited with Tom's father almost seven years earlier. It had been one of the most memorable holidays of my life.

We had rented a villa for two weeks from one of his work colleagues – one of his very wealthy work colleagues. The villa overlooked the medieval walled city of Lucca, famous for both its olive oil (it is one of Sainsbury's major suppliers) and its night time candlelit procession through the streets in summer.

We had a hill-top view of the city from our villa. It had ten bedrooms, and a large flag-stone floored kitchen, with an Aga that for once didn't look out of place. One bathroom, if you opened the windows from your bath, gave you a unique 'room with a view' – even Helena Bonham Carter and Maggie Smith would have been envious.

Each evening, we partied late into the night, lighting candles around the pool, drinking fine wines and eating even finer foods as we watched the festivities in Lucca. We drank and ate with the neighbours and listened to Pavarotti blaring out from the mustard yellow Lotus Elan Tom's father owned. (Three years later, I wrote off this un-baby friendly car by wrapping it round a tree, narrowly missing a rabbit.)

****

This time I arrived at the villa with Tom in tow. The road to the villa had always been steep and poorly maintained. No Lotus now, but the Golf GTi manoeuvred well and dealt with the hairpin bends up the hill with relative ease.

The place was exactly as I remembered it. Grand villa, spectacular views – and sunshine. Tom was not impressed with the sun or the villa, and made it known he wanted shade and to be indoors. The flag stones in the kitchen made it an ideal place to perch him in his travel cot.

The villa had a nursery but I had failed to notice this on my previous visit. I hadn't even bothered to open the nursery door. I wasn't a maternal woman before Tom's birth. There had been no biological clock, no tick-tock. Like many women on the London Underground I found the sight and sound of babies irritating unless they were either very attractive, very well-behaved or both. Now the shoe was firmly and eternally on the other foot. I understood exactly why I got the glares and the sighs that I had, I am now ashamed to say, given in my childless state.

But in Italy it was different. There were no glares and the only sighs were ones of admiration. My first trip into Lucca says it all. It was a Wednesday morning and a market day.

The square in medieval Lucca is packed at any time of the year; in June it is just starting to warm up for the tourists, but has not yet gathered full momentum. There is an air of expectancy, the anticipation of great things to come. Lots of money will be spent. That hasn't happened yet, but it will: it does every year.

I decided to take Tom down the hill to town in the car and then use the pushchair rather than the front carrier. It was getting warmer, and although the carrier is ideal in a cool climate, as it had been in France, in Lucca it was starting to get hot. So with foldaway pushchair, parasol and little linen outfit for Tom, and a matching one for me (OK, I had bought something matching in La Baule after all), we headed into town.

I went to Lucca with the intention of getting provisions for the rest of the week – food and cleaning stuff, and perhaps a toy for Tom, something that would remind me of my visit to Lucca with him even if it would not have any memory value for Tom himself. I thought I would try to buy something for him in each place we visited together.

Unless you are a resident, you are not permitted to drive in Lucca. You park outside the town in a large car park surrounded by cobblestones and ornate archways. All the various points of entry lead to the square where the market is held each day. The sound of voices guides you as you walk through the narrow lanes. The tall buildings on either side are well preserved, with ornate balconies, flower baskets, and the occasional line of washing. (Often these are festooned with white sheets but also white, black and red frilly knickers. Interesting lot, these Luccans.)

Tom was as fascinated as I was by the surroundings. His eyes darted from one face to another as quickly as the flies had danced around Fred the donkey's head back in M. Guillet's vineyard.

Restaurant waiters were starting to put tables and chairs out for the al fresco customers of the day, and these made an interesting obstacle course for Tom's buggy.

He seemed to enjoy the bumping over cobblestones and the swerving in and out of chairs and tables, of the locals going about their business. The shop windows were alternately full of designer flares at designer prices and the smoked meats and cheeses of the local grocers. Then we arrived in the main square, the hive of activity.

There must have been a hundred stalls selling everything from leather goods to groceries, from tourist trinkets to hardware which only the locals would buy and know how to use. The customers were mainly women. Like the shops, they were a mixture of slender designer chic and comfortable, motherly types. The motherly types looked like those dolls – the 'weebles' – that always wobble but don't fall down.

Tom was delighted with it all. At every opportunity, he giggled and laughed and gave himself hiccups. The little boy fascinated the Luccans. Several times, we caused traffic jams as women would come up and bend over to stroke his hair, tweak his cheek or even pull him out of the buggy and give him a big bear hug. Singing to him seemed to be the most fashionable way of making him respond. Anything by Pavarotti, all vaguely reminiscent of O Sole Mio seemed to do the trick. Meanwhile he giggled and laughed and hiccuped in unison with their tunes.

I wondered if they did this to every baby that came to the market. I didn't see any other babies with their mothers, and in my broken Italian asked one of the bear-hugging weebles if all babies were treated in such a way.

'Ah, yes. We love babies. But women don't tend to bring their babies to the market because it causes such problems. Congestion.'

Eventually, I decided to buy some of the local produce, finding that having Tom in tow meant I was usually given a pound or two more of everything 'for the bambino'.

My shopping done, I thought I would take Tom for a walk round the streets I had visited before with his father. With a pushchair in front, I realised that some streets would now prove impassable, which was a pity. But at least the buggy was a foldaway one. So, determined to go where I had been before, I carried Tom under one arm, and the buggy under the other. OK, so he saw the street from a lop sided point of view, but he didn't seem to mind. Instead of looking at people's knees, at least he was able to look them in the face.

A café on the corner of one of the narrow streets beckoned. There were tables and chairs outside, with a reassuring number of people eating and drinking and no English voices. Though it was in the sun, each table had a parasol, so I could do my contortionist trick of keeping Tom in the shade and me in the rays.

I sat at a spare table. The proprietor came over and asked if I wanted more room for the buggy. No, I was fine. Was I sure? Yes, I was sure. The couple at the next table would be happy to move if I wanted more room. No I was fine, honest I was. Tom was fine. He was giggling, laughing and hiccuping as ever.

He definitely seemed to be enjoying his first trip to Italy.

What would I like? This part of Italy is famous for its beans. In fact in neighbouring parts of Italy they call the Luccans 'bean eaters'. If you are vegetarian, it's a good place to go. Their bean soup is particularly good, and that is what I decided to have. Would the baby like anything, the waiter asked. No, he was fine. He was on tap.

Did any food need to be warmed up? No, that wasn't necessary. Was I sure? Yes, I was sure. Really? Yes, really. Was my son too hot? No, he was fine.

As I sat soaking up the sun, with my bean soup and my local white, light and fruity wine, my son soaked up the attention of the local women. The chic, skinny ones and the comfortable motherly types. The men were just as tactile with him, although they paid more attention to me than the women. The women would open their handbags and jiggle bundles of keys in front of him. I wondered if that was their method of seducing older men as well. Tom liked playing with keys, as I think all babies do.

Italians seem to have an instinct about how to handle and talk to babies. They seem completely at ease in their company, almost as though it is more natural to have a baby in tow than not to have one. At the risk of sounding incredibly corny, somehow, having brought Tom to Lucca, I felt more complete this time.

Because of the attention Tom attracted, I found myself entering into conversations and finding out much more about the locals and their way of life than I would have done as a journalist with a tape recorder, microphone and brief in hand. Perhaps Tom would prove to be my secret weapon in getting under the skin of the place and the people I met on my professional travels, although I would probably have to give the white water rafting and bungee jumping a miss.

As a journalist, I had always found Italians happy to talk. But they would more readily and easily answer questions when Tom was doing his hiccup trick in their laps. The fact that he had already developed a winning smile also helped.

Tom was and is a flirt. He would smile and flutter his long eye lashes and both the Italian women and men would be like putty in his hands. Occasionally he might throw up over their designer shirts or skirts, but that was irrelevant. He was a pretty baby, as even the most critical and cynical would agree.

He still has blue eyes and blond hair. His mother and father, alas, both have dark hair, though I am a persistent peroxide offender. Perhaps some of it seeped into the womb, because Tom has hair as fair as anything out of a bottle. He also has blue eyes like his father and I pray that they stay that way. Babies often have blue eyes until 12 months, and then overnight they turn to a sludgy brown or green. As mine are sludgy browny green, I am anticipating the change any day.

I used to pray a wish list for Tom every night. Still do. I pray he maintains incredibly good health and never has to enter a hospital. That he has eternal happiness. That he has the wisdom of Solomon. That he has spiritual, mental, emotional and physical strength – that he keeps those big blue eyes. He kept them for Lucca anyway.

Appropriately enough, Tom also discovered the power of pulling in Italy. I'm not talking pulling as in the emotional sense – although he undoubtedly made many friends that day – but pulling as in pulling at anything within arms' reach. That included hair, earrings, noses, lips, eyebrows, cufflinks, table cloths. Anything that wasn't nailed down, he would pull it. Strong little arms Tom had.

Another recommendation for you. Tom is not an intentional kleptomaniac. But shops which have little gifts on open view are easy targets for a baby who has just discovered the delights of picking up and pulling at things and sticking them in his mouth. When so much is going on around you, it's easy to forget what is within arms' reach. I learnt the hard way in a shop which was selling leather bracelets and handbags. The goods were laid out on neat little circular tables, at just the right level for a baby in a buggy to lean over and grab. Perhaps overwhelmed by the hospitality and ease of the baby-friendly Luccans, I left Tom for a moment to look at a handbag which was screaming 'buy me' from the wall. Having given in to temptation, I returned to Tom to discover he had half the contents of the table in his lap, and some in his mouth, up his nose, in his hair and one, inexplicably, down his trousers. I apologised to the shop assistant (who luckily found the whole event hilariously funny and proceeded to make Tom giggle) and put all the fashionable leather goods back on the table. Then we made a speedy exit before the assistant was able to bear-hug my son into a frenzy of hiccups. Some shops may not be so understanding, so beware.

****

After our week in Lucca, self catering in a large luxury villa, I decided to move south to the remote towns and villages of the Cinque Terre. To my utter amazement, it is still relatively unknown and unspoiled. I had previously visited the area as a tour guide, when I was 21. I had left school at 18, after achieving disappointing A-level results. At that stage, I knew only that I loved travelling and nothing else. I needed time to think what I wanted to do. It was not like today when every self-respecting five-year-old knows they want to be a television presenter or a Spice Girl – or be married to one.

Really I needed to go to university or college to give me time to think. But my cousin worked for Barclays International and had travelled extensively through her work. She had lived in Fiji, Manila and Hong Kong, and I loved the sound of these exotic places. Also the bank paid for everything. So banking it was. I joined the Midland Bank (now part of HSBC) at the bottom rung. I hated it. I hated every moment of it. I hated my first day and hated my last. I stuck it out for three years, every day of which I hated. I would cry each morning, and my mother would scold me saying very few people enjoy what they do for a living, but that I had to be responsible for once in my life and earn my keep. I wondered if everyone cried each morning the way I did.

I left after 1096 days, 4 hours and 20 minutes. Approximately. I didn't have a job to go to, so I made one up just to save face. 'Something in PR', I told my colleagues. They gave me some cut glass as a going-away present and signed a big card with blessings they didn't mean. I've kept the card and still have one of the glasses.

While I was temping, doing 'something in PR', I noticed an advertisement in *The Times* for tour guides for a small upmarket independent travel company which organises exclusive tours around the loveliest parts of Europe: through the Dordogne, the Loire, the road to Rome, unknown Umbria, Spoleto, over the Dolomites, to Verona, and Venice. And to an area called the Cinque Terre.

The Cinque Terre, or five lands as it literally translates, is on the west coast of Italy, north of Tuscany. It is unspoiled and beautiful.

Difficult to explore by car, it is ideal for walking – you reach each coastal town along spectacular coastal paths. Some, though not all, are clearly marked. There is also a charming coastal train.

This company took groups of about 12 cash rich, time poor 25- to 55-year-old travellers through the five lands. Two guides hosted each group. One would lead the party each day, while the other would take the luggage in a Land Rover to the next hotel.

I believe they were one of the first companies to specialise in what the travel industry now calls 'soft adventure', where travellers trek without luggage in the wilderness, blazing trails no one has blazed before, in the expectation of a wonderful ready prepared picnic at lunch time and five star or equivalent accommodation at the end of each day. It was and is a wonderful idea – and unsurprisingly the company is thriving to this day.

Probably to their infinite regret, they hired me to guide several groups in the Cinque Terre that autumn. My Italian was rusty but I had an easy manner and was eager to learn and make friends. I worked with a girl called Elianna, who was fun and intelligent and spoke Italian as her native language, whilst her English was better than most English people's. She drove and I led the group.

The first day of the first week, I got the group lost. Admittedly I had not been shown the route first hand and was given only rough written directions. But it was still a poor show when I had to admit in front of my group – who were a bunch of professional 30- and 40-something high powered, demanding achievers, each of whom had paid a lot of money to come on the trip – that I didn't know where we were.

'I think we've taken a wrong turn. I think we should retrace our steps', I winced, as we struggled down a steep bank which looked particularly dead-ended. Eventually Elianna picked us up halfway down the hill, scowling at me and apologising to the group. I felt dreadful, and spent most of the evening apologising profusely to everyone for getting it wrong. For being there. For being alive. For being me. You get the picture.

The next day, I led the group (who were now a little more cautious about following me) on the second stretch of the journey. I had not practised this bit before but thankfully didn't get them lost. They all seemed grateful, as well as surprised and relieved.

Each lunch-time, Elianna would greet us in the olive grove, or vineyard, or forest which had been pre-selected as the place we would meet her. Each morning the guests prepared for their mystery tour led by Sarah, who was just as in the dark about the route as they were. Elianna would have been to the local market and bought the local produce: fruit, wine, cheese, smoked meats and hams, and mineral water. This would be laid out on a large blanket as she awaited our arrival with a smile, a bottle in one hand and cups in the other. She was a lovely person to know and work with.

On the fourth day, God decreed there would be rain. Lots of it. I led the group through wind and rain and kept smiling and thankfully didn't get them lost. But they never forgave me for the first day, and left me with only a small tip and rather a lot of ill feeling.

By the second week, I was more in tune with where to go and what to do. The group was also much more friendly and a lot of them already knew each other. There were judges and solicitors and journalists, and people who would climb every mountain and follow every stream. It was then that I grew to love this part of the world and the work. The confidence the first group had damaged, the second group restored.

I only did the trip for two weeks. My flat was burgled during the third so I had to return home. Thus it was with mixed feelings that I returned to the Cinque Terre with Tom. The place had ghosts for me and I wanted to dispel them.

I wanted to see if I could walk the same paths with Tom. The views had been spectacular and the thought of being completely at one with nature, away from the city and busy urban life, was attractive after the bustle of Lucca.

The five lands are: Monterosso al Mare, Vernazza, Corniglia, Manarola and Riomaggiore.

Each is quaint, unspoiled, charming.

We stayed in Levanto the first night, before starting our trip to the first of the five lands – Monterosso. The medieval walled town of Levanto has palm trees along narrow medieval alleys and buildings which date from the eighth century. Tom was oblivious to this. All he cared about was that the family run, neo-classical hotel, Hotel Nazionale, provided a cot, a private garden with shade and a very warm welcome for both him and his mum.

On this trip I didn't have the benefit of an Elianna carrying the luggage for me. I had to travel light as I was on my own. Previously I had taken a few hours each day to complete each section of the journey. With Tom I would be slower, and he would grow tired and need a rest every so often, even if I didn't.

He was still quite light, at about 12 pounds in his stockinged feet. I carried only the bare essentials, mostly his, in my backpack. The trail was quite well marked between Levanto and Monterosso. It cut up and down hillsides and through olive groves. There was no idyllic picnic awaiting my arrival this time, but there were no tourists either, and I could go at my own peaceful pace.

I heard only the chirping of crickets as I made my way over streams, through vines, and along the coastal path. I had forgotten how narrow it was in places, even without a baby in harness. I was pleased that it was Spring, when the weather, though warm, lacked the intense heat of high summer.

Two hours into the journey, I arrived in a small field of lavender, where I remember Elianna had organised one of the picnics. I unhooked Thomas from the carrier and put him down gently under the shade of a tree.

He was sleepy and thirsty. I picked him up and nursed him, perched up against the trunk, very quietly looking down at him as he looked back up at me. I felt very peaceful and calm sitting with my son, as I thought back to how tense I had been on my previous journey to that part of the world. I remembered how desperate I had been to impress the troops and not to let them down.

The path had become well-trodden over the years and as I nursed Tom, a few other groups, perhaps with Alternative Travel who still organise unguided trips along this coast, walked past me. Smiling. Nodding good day. The English walkers seemed to be embarrassed by the sight·of a young woman feeding her baby. They said 'good afternoon' and scuttled past quickly. The Italians, on the other hand, just smiled and went on their way.

Vernazza is the second of the five lands. I remember it being very busy and bustling on my first journey, and it hadn't changed. As Tom was awake and seemed eager, I decided to continue our journey on to Manarola and Riomaggiore and get a room in the latter for the night. There was no room at the Villa Argentina, with sea views at the top of the village, where the group had stayed before, but there was room at a nearby restaurant with rooms above. The proprietor said he didn't have a cot, but that he would see what he could do. The room, though small, was very clean, and the man brought in a small wooden cot, saying that it belonged to a neighbour who no longer had need of it. 'Babies are always welcome here', he said.

He went on to say that he would be happy to bring my food up to my room if this helped, but I replied that I would prefer to eat early if possible, and eat in the restaurant. No problem. The man showed Tom and me to a table outside, under a large parasol. The table had a large bottle of mineral water and two glasses. The proprietor, a Signor Umberto, had lived in the village all his life. He spoke good English and told me he had seen many English people walking the trail I had just taken, but never anyone with a baby.

I explained to him what I was doing with Tom: travelling with him as much as I could in his first year. He thought this was a good idea, but to embark on such a journey one had to be fit and healthy and take extra precautions. He didn't think travelling by myself with Tom was a good idea in this part of the world, and that it would have been better if I had had a guide with me.

In retrospect, I agree with Signor Umberto, but this part of the trip was one of the rare occasions when it would be just the two of us. For this reason, if for no other, it was special.

I slept like the proverbial log, and so did Tom: in fact we didn't wake until 10 am, which is unheard of. After a light breakfast, we headed for the next town of Portovenere.

This part of the coastal path is spectacular when the sun shines. I had encountered storms and heavy rains there on my first trip but had kept smiling through despite feeling miserable. With Tom, everything seemed so much more beautiful and alive. Before, I had had to focus on following the right route, finding Elianna's picnic place, and getting to our destination before nightfall, but this time the trail was clearly signposted and I was able to enjoy the natural surroundings with a sense of peace, and serenity.

Since giving birth I felt I had slowed down. I couldn't be in so much of a rush, even in London. I had to take my time and consider Tom's well being. I had to protect his small body in busy, crowded places. By the time I reached Portovenere, through the terraced vineyards, my thoughts couldn't have been further from London's aggressive streets.

I had forgotten how steep the last part of the journey was. It was almost as though someone had placed flagstones on the side of a hill, and one had to walk in between them. The only way I thought I could do this part of the journey was on my backside. It may not have looked ladylike, but it seemed the safest way to me. So, just as a baby does when he learns to crawl, I bottom-wobbled my way down. It was a wonderful treatment for cellulite and Tom found it highly amusing, as did the locals who came to look at the spectacle of this weird lady with her baby.

By the time I reached the bottom, a young girl was waiting for me with a glass of cold lemonade. She smiled and gave me the glass, and said something which sounded friendly but which I didn't understand. The dialect in these parts was very strong. I drank from the glass in the hope it wasn't poison. You never know – the girl could have been a relative of one of the tourists I had led in the first group all those years ago.

LESSONS LEARNT IN ITALY

1.   Remember how you felt about babies before you had one yourself
If you can, that is. My experience on the London Underground may have been particularly poor, but I must admit, I was not considerate when I saw other mothers with young babies and pushchairs when I had a deadline to meet in London. Mothers with pushchairs obviously take up a lot of space – other people's space – and they have rights too. If you are considerate with how you ask for help, rather than expecting it, you may find other travellers are more helpful and considerate in their attitude towards you.

2.   Toys overseas
Although there are now European rules and regulations dictating what is and what isn't a safe toy, always be very aware of safety factors when buying toys overseas for your baby (especially cute fluffy ones which may have eyes which easily come out and can be swallowed). Keep mementoes simple: perhaps ones that can be appreciated when the child is older.

3.   See with the baby's eyes
Think of what your baby sees when you are travelling with him. The beauty of a front carrier, especially if the child is facing forwards, is that he sees other faces. In a pushchair, all he will see is people's knees. Of course, as babies get older, they get heavier, and a front carrier becomes a problem. That's another reason why it is best to travel when they are so young.

4. Conversation starters

In my experience, babies are marvellous conversation starters. People will talk to you and to your baby, especially in countries like Italy. As I learnt in France, baby talk is a universal language.

6. Don't go OTT

If you are taking a walking holiday with a baby in tow, check the climate (not too hot, nor too cold), and that the journey has sufficient stops for breaks and offers shade and is well routed. (For example, the Cinque Terre coastal path is well trodden, but with a baby there are parts which are best taken by the coastal train – which is just as much fun and quicker.) Be adventurous but within reason. Stay close to towns and cities where the health facilities are accessible and available. I am advocating getting out and about more, not taking your baby to some place you would think twice about going to yourself.

SWEDEN AND FINLAND

Four Months

I wasn't really looking forward to travelling to Stockholm. At the time I was working as a media consultant for an advertising agency. Actually, that sounds rather grand: let me explain.

I was not earning enough money to support my work as a reporter for Classic FM, and I needed a more reliable income as well. An opportunity arose to work for an outdoor advertising company (billboards and bus shelters – sexy huh?) as their public relations manager. I had just finished presenting a television series 'Who's been sleeping in my bed?', which I had devised, interviewing celebrities such as Sir Terence Conran, Lord Menuhin and Sir David Frost, plus any other titled traveller who cared to discuss their favourite hotels around the world. The series was shown on a station called European

Business News that no longer exists. It was heady stuff but didn't pay any bills, so this was an opportunity to earn some money and do a 'proper' job.

At the advertising agency, I worked long hours, enjoyed little home life, lost a lot of weight (which was good) and suffered from a stream of stinking colds (which was bad). The upside to the job was the people, who were absolutely wonderful, inspirational and a pleasure to see each morning. They were the best people I have ever met or had the pleasure to work with. The boss was incredibly dynamic, a great motivator whose enthusiasm was infectious. Even for billboards and bus shelters.

But I had the travel bug. I wanted to continue to travel through work. I had travelled extensively for Classic FM, visiting many different countries. The travel for the advertising company would be different, ostensibly to see another businessman in another office in another country, but it would be business-class all the way and I would be earning, too. Thus I could combine work with my ultimate pleasure – travelling.

My first port of call was Stockholm. I had never been to Sweden for Classic FM although I had visited neighbouring Finland. The Finns didn't seem to like the Swedes much. Those I spoke to thought the Swedish a bit wild and brash.

I didn't really get to know the Swedes very well on this brief excursion to its capital but the place seemed pleasant enough. I gave myself enough time to look around the city which is remarkably and unexpectedly beautiful. The people are not all blond and beautiful, but they are friendly and seem to be very at ease with themselves and life in general.

The weather was pretty grey on the days I was there, but unlike in London, when on grey days you see nothing but grey faces, everyone in Stockholm seemed to be oblivious to the dark clouds.

The flight had been quick and efficient: two and a half hours from London Heathrow to Arlanda. The business class service on SAS (Scandinavian Airlines) was immaculate and the cabin almost empty. I was offered everyone else's allocated half bottle of champagne and decided to take it for the troops back home. The airport was busy but the taxi rank was easy to find. The meeting was long and productive and the hotel into which I had been booked was modern and business-like, right in the centre of town. The entire first floor was designated as a dining-room providing breakfasts catering for all nationalities, from American to English to Japanese, to Scandinavian to goodness-knows-what. If you had any particular fancy that morning they would have been able to cater for it.

There were plenty of shops in the business district and many of the streets were pedestrianised so I could walk and browse with ease.

****

On my journey to Sweden second time round, Tom had just turned four months and had now received his first injections.

The international airport, Arlanda, is 25 miles outside Stockholm itself. Arlanda is not particularly easy to find your way around, but people were helpful and every shop had a child friendly assistant who would be happy to hold, feed, burp and change Thomas while I hunted for the cheapest smoked salmon and pickled herrings I could find.

Every shop seems to sell smoked salmon and smoked oysters as well as little trolls, which would have scared Tom if he had been old enough to focus and know what they were. I bought him one with a bright pink tuft on its head. But Tom was at the stick-everything-in-your-mouth stage. You know, live wire, plug, knife, pin, scissors – and the troll's head was but another object to explore. He sucked most of the hair off in the first few days in Stockholm, and the troll looked even meaner as a skinhead with what looked like a pink, heart-shaped tattoo left where the tuft had been.

The streets of Stockholm were buzzing mid-morning, mid week. A mishmash of shoppers and businessmen were busy rushing to the next meeting, shop, affair, as Tom and I hailed a cab.

The taxi driver was from Stockholm. (Unlike New York, where I don't think there is a single taxi driver who is from the United States, let alone the Big Apple.)

This Swedish person didn't like living there. He wanted to live in England. He liked England. No, he had never been there. Most people who like England have never been there. They seem to believe in the myth of the streets being paved with gold, or at least in the existence of the English gent and the buttered scone, and the genteel civility of English life as described in Agatha Christie's Miss Marple novels. I tried to set the taxi driver straight.

'I come from just outside London. It's a dirty city, and people are impatient and inconsiderate – especially when you have a baby in tow. It's not a good place to take children. What's Stockholm like?'

'Ah, we love babies here. Yes, we love babies. Very practical though. No romance about babies. I have four. When you have four, you have no romance about babies.'

I had one and I had no romance about babies either, I thought.

'When women work and have a baby, they are well looked after. They can go back to work and not lose any money and that is good. But Sweden is good with all people. We are good with the mentally ill and people who are in prison as well. We look after them well.'

Mothers grouped with those who were mentally ill and criminals, eh? Perhaps the Swedish were similar to the English after all, I thought.

'How old is your son, four months?'

'Yes, four months, exactly.'

'Ah, fathers can tell. When you have four babies you can tell. Boy or girl?'

Obviously he wasn't that good.

'Boy.'

'Name?'

'Tom. Thomas. Thomas Edward Benjamin.'

'Good name. Good names. You choose?'

'Yes, we both had a say.'

'What are your children called?' I asked him.

I won't even try to write the taxi driver's reply. I couldn't even spell what he said phonetically. Let's just say, even the abbreviations would have had three syllables. Whatever happened to names like Sven and Britt?

We arrived at the hotel after a drive which took about half an hour. The hotel was a large one, purpose-built for businessmen, and didn't seem on the face of it at all suitable for mothers with babies. But how wrong I was.

As soon as I entered the foyer, the doorman ushered me in, insisting almost to the point of aggression on taking my bags. Two female receptionists – both striking, both blonde – grinned at Thomas. He, astute even at four months, grinned back.

I was only staying for one night, but they treated me as though I was staying for a month. A cot? I hadn't ordered one. No worries, there would be one. Wooden, was that OK? Did I want to go out that night? They had a nanny service at no extra cost. No I didn't, but thank you.

There was a range of baby food on the menu or they could mash up adult food. Thomas looked about four months (these Swedes were good at guessing ages – I wondered if they were as accurate with mine), so I was probably still breast-feeding. (I was, but my cleavage was nothing compared to that of the Swedish receptionists. No wonder Tom grinned.) Was Tom allergic to anything? They had goat's milk or soya milk in stock if cow's milk was not appropriate.

I asked the porter who showed me to my room (on the first floor, by the lift, so not far to walk), why this business hotel of all places was so well equipped to handle women with babies.

'We have a lot of women on business staying here who bring their babies with them. Sometimes they have their nannies, but most of the women who come here are regulars and when they have babies, we just adapt and so do they. It's a service which is easy to provide and we like babies here.'

The hotel also provided a crèche (the size of my whole ground floor at home), and nannies who could speak many languages, including Japanese. They could even speak (like the Italians and French) the universal 'language of Tom' – which at the age of four months consisted of 'coo, coo, coo' and occasionally 'ahhhhhhh'.

My room was clean and large; the cot was clean and large too, and safe, and better than the one he has at home. Unlike the soaps and mouth washes, unfortunately, I couldn't cram it into my suitcase.

Rather than eat in, I decided to venture out on foot, asking for a good restaurant which would be appropriate for Tom and me.

'Any restaurant is able to cater for you. Some are better than others, but all are good. Do you want me to book one for you?'

'Yes, please.'

'Italian, Swedish, French, Japanese, English?'

'Swedish, please.' When in Rome ...

The heavily bosomed blonde receptionist picked up the phone, dialled and said something lacking in vowels and violently guttural into the receiver. After two minutes she put it down, smiled, gave me directions and told me they were expecting me. And Tom.

The walk to the restaurant was lovely. Considering we were in the centre of a busy city, Stockholm is a remarkably beautiful place. Built on a string of islands, the city was founded 700 years ago by King

Birger Jarl where the fresh water of Lake Malaren meets the salt water of the Baltic. (It's true. I read it on the plane.) I found myself in Stockholm's commercial area and yet it still looked clean and the people all seemed very friendly and contented and though in a hurry, not in too much of one to smile at passers-by.

The restaurant looked busy – too busy and noisy for a mother with a baby was my initial thought. I nearly turned back in search of a Pizza Express – guaranteed to be good with babies wherever they are. But no. I entered. A man came to greet us. He spoke excellent English with the merest trace of an accent, which was quite endearing. This was completely lost on Tom, but not on his mother.

'Tom is four months old, yes?' (That age thing again: these Swedish are good.) 'Too young for a high chair – we have a mini-cot we could put him down in. I expect he is not sitting up yet. Back not strong enough.' (Did this guy have four babies too?)

We were led to a table which was not tucked away in the corner, away from everyone else; we sat by the window, with a wonderful view of the shoppers busy shopping.

I was handed a menu and told if I wanted to feed Thomas myself, that was no problem. In fact, the waiter (whose name was Sven – thank goodness) pointed to another woman who was feeding her child at the time.

'We're very open about breast-feeding in Sweden – it's natural. The English are a bit touchy about their boobs, aren't they?' said Sven.

Couldn't have put it better myself.

I ordered smoked salmon and poached salmon and if there had been a salmon dessert I would have ordered that as well, but just chose camomile tea instead. The restaurant had a variety of customers: courting couples, families, businessmen, girlfriends chatting over tea and cakes, or pickled herring or smoked salmon perhaps. For once it was nice to feel part of the human race, not segregated into a place intended only for women with babies.

****

I didn't know what to expect when I got to Finland.

My last visit there had been made in winter. Just before one Christmas, on an assignment for Classic FM, I had flown to Helsinki from London (just under three hours and very efficient) with Finnair, and then north to Rovaniemi. I had been commissioned to produce a feature, on among other things, the Northern Lights, Santapark and the ice-breaker Sampo. The Sampo had been turned into a corporate hospitality ship, where groups of businessmen and women could have an ice-cold jolly on an iced-over river.

I like the Finns. They have an affinity with the Japanese, in that both nationalities are incredibly inscrutable. They don't speak much or give much away and have this dreadful habit of always thinking before they speak. Never trust anyone who has the sense to think before they speak. They never mean what they say.

The Finnish language is also one of the most impossible to learn. Only real Finns can speak Finnish, which forces them to learn other languages and so most are incredible linguists. Japanese and Finnish are the two most difficult languages in the world to learn, the Finnair in-flight magazine informed me. Listen to anyone speaking Finnish and you will know why. Thankfully, most Finns speak good to excellent English or French or German or Spanish.

At the time of this assignment, I had decided to dye my hair a very white shade of blonde. My hair is dead straight. There is no wave, no curl, and no crinkle in it. It hangs, motionless, fine and soft and bloody awful to do anything with. My natural colour is a rather nasty shade of brown. For the past ten years the hair had undergone so many transformations of perm and colour and colour on perm, and heated tong bob, that it had almost fallen out. On the Finland trip it was returning to its normal texture, soft, dead straight, but white blonde.

I have a wide, round moon-face, wide-set eyes, wide mouth and pert little nose. I looked Finnish. I know I looked Finnish because the usually quiet Finns all spoke to me and when they did, they spoke to me in Finnish. They told me I looked Finnish. By the end of the trip, I felt part of a mysterious club which I had been allowed into by dint of looking like everyone else. Believe it or not, there are lots of people who look like me in Finland. I quizzed my mother about my parentage when I returned home but she insisted I had no Finnish blood in me – unless of course an ancestor of my father's had been subject to a bit of rape and pillage by Vikings at some stage.

Finland in winter is very cold: minus 20 when I was there. The guide was so annoying: she kept telling me 'It's very warm for this time of year'. Yeah, right.

The Northern Lights are spectacular. The legends behind them are various and none of them do I really believe. But they are something to tell the children, which the Finns like to do in great detail. To some it is good luck to see them, to others they bring bad luck, but I wanted to see them anyway. These streaks of colour move across the sky so quickly, they seem almost to overpower it. They look like dancing waves of light, wafting like feathery flames across a sky which hangs like a blank canvas to show them off. It is a weird and wonderful experience, well worth the effort.

On my first day in Finland I took a snowmobile across a frozen lake. I didn't know that's what it was until I was right in the middle of it. My Finnish guide, who was on the machine in front of me, told me to be very careful to follow in her tracks as some of the ice was weak and I might fall through. God did I stick to that woman's butt after that.

After about half a mile we were scheduled to meet a man at a certain time with his reindeer. This traditional and slower way to travel was also very uncomfortable, very smelly and very cold. Reindeer, like huskies, I found, all seem to suffer from dreadful wind. It always looks so nice on films, but being at the same level as the reindeer's backside has just about as much appeal as being behind a group of huskies. However, we jingled our way through the snow to a log cabin, where I tasted some very potent glühwein and got quite heady with the cold, lack of food and too much alcohol. I had put on about ten layers of clothing before I had left for the journey and still felt the cold trying to bite through.

I looked almost as big then as I did in the last few days before I had Tom.

****

Ah, Tom. Tom at four months, and 20 degrees below on a good day? No, I wouldn't take Tom to Finland in the winter. In the spring, maybe, when the heat of the sun was starting to warm things up and the days were longer and the mosquitoes had yet to sink their teeth into the natives and stray tourists.

In the spring, Finland was a completely different proposition. In the winter, the all-day darkness made it eternally cosy with log fires the main source of warmth and light. In the spring, the Finns like to get naked in their wood-stove saunas. They are a tough breed. They fought and defeated the Russians, as they are always proud to tell you, and they think nothing of sleeping in igloos, on ice beds in ice castles and ice hotels which they build every November and which melt every spring.

There was no snow in April. But I wanted to visit Santapark, which had been launched by the Finnish Tourist Board as the definitive home of Father Christmas. The North Pole, Sweden, Iceland and Finland have fought for decades over who owns the rights to Santa's birthplace.

The Finns have always tried to do this bigger, better and properly: they have turned a nuclear fall-out shelter into Santa's grotto. Sounds dreadful doesn't it? But the idea that it should be the safest place on earth, where Santa is supposed to make all your dreams come true (which could reasonably include, 'please could I survive a nuclear war') perhaps make it an ideal location for his home.

You enter this enormous bunker by train and there you walk through various 'lands' where elves and fairies are all busy doing something, but you never know what. There are lots of colours and lights and images of woods and sweets and toys, and basically everything that could lighten up any young face – and even turn a cynical old journalist into a believer in fairies. (I am, I am.)

I did take Tom to have a look, but he was unimpressed. At the age of four months, I suppose I shouldn't have expected more. It was all a blur of colour and noise and smell to him, but he smiled, which was nice. I liked it and thought I would bring him back when he was, say, four years older. He might also appreciate the reindeer then, and the glorious countryside and the friendly but quiet Finns, who, like the Swedes, 'like babies'.

Tom was too young to go in a sauna (although I was desperate for one) and I kept him clear of the huskies, because the ones I saw looked rather hungry. Even the ice-breaker-turned-cruise-ship, the Sampo, which on my original trip I had ventured onto with a group of Spanish chemists (I kid you not), was not in operation because, in the spring, there is no ice.

But it was good to return to this country and see again the people I had met when I had been single, on business. Now they looked at me in a different way, as a visitor who had chosen to return, without an agenda or a microphone, and at their own rather than someone else's expense. Everyone I met said how much Tom looked like me. How much he looked like a Finn.

LESSONS LEARNT IN SWEDEN AND FINLAND

1. Climate

Be careful with the climate, as when travelling anywhere with a baby: too cold is as bad as too hot. Go in the spring and autumn when the mosquitoes aren't as active and the temperatures not as extreme. Wherever you go always take into account the time of year you are travelling and the temperatures involved. For example, Dubai has excellent hotels which offer great facilities for families travelling with babies, but February is the best time to go as it is relatively cooler (in the 60's and 70's Fahrenheit). Don't go later on when temperatures reach the 80's, 90's and beyond. You may be able to take it but your baby can't.

2. Travel for yourself

Travel for yourself, not for your baby. You – his mum or dad – are the centre of his world. Choose a list of five destinations and hotels you want to go to, and check that they cater for a young baby. You will be pleasantly surprised by their response. Remember the only thing your baby really needs at that age is you.

3. Breast-feeding in public

Cultural differences vary enormously. Scandinavians are very relaxed about breast-feeding in public, but in certain places in the States it is a jailable offence – although America, in general, is very good if you are travelling with a baby.

4. Travelling as a single parent

I did most of my travelling without my other half – he didn't have the time to come with me. I found empathy between mother and baby grows on your travels when there are only the two of you. If you carry your baby around in a front carrier, you feel as one most of the time.

AUSTRIA

Four Months

I don't like skiing. Very uncool to say so, I know, but I don't. I am fit, flexible, but as my ski instructor in Mayerhofen said when I took my first lesson, 'You have very strong muscles but you are scared shit, yes?'

Yes, I was scared shit. I was also very cold all the time. Learning to ski is a bit like learning to play tennis. Once you can get the ball over the net, you have so much more fun. When you're learning, all you seem to do is pick up balls. When you're learning to ski, all you seem to do is pick yourself up from the ground. Or at least, try to.

The visit to Mayerhofen wasn't my first trip to Austria. I had been to Innsbruck on one of my father's school trips when I was about six. There was me and thirty boys, all between the ages of 14 and 16. The

trip had involved lots of cultural visits which bored the boys, but there had also been great competition between Dad's school and another English boys' school staying in an adjacent hotel. The girls of the town were certainly very happy and preoccupied that winter.

The second time I went to Austria was on an 18-30 holiday with a friend who was a nurse. She preferred the après ski to the skiing. While I traipsed up and down those mountains in Mayerhofen, she was quite content to snow plough on the nursery slopes chatting up the instructor.

We started off as a group of ten beginners. I had bought my first ski outfit ever (an all-in-one, bright turquoise number from C & A) and I looked disgusting. Ski boots and skis I hired on location. On the first day I took someone else's ski boots by mistake and walked to the lifts in boots too tight. By the time I got to the top, my instructor realised my mistake and told me to return to the bottom. By this time, my shins were cut and bleeding, my ankles red raw; that evening I could barely walk. The thought of putting those boots – any boots – back on again made me feel sick. Added to that it was very cold, I kept falling over and I couldn't master parallel turns. I would start off in one direction and just keep heading that way until I ran out of mountain, then fall to one side, shuffle round on my bum until I was facing in the opposite direction, then push myself up with my sticks in an ungainly fashion and start the process all over again.

Eventually I would reach the bottom of the mountain, but it was very slow and very dull. A bit like hitting tennis balls against a wall in order to improve your strokes but always hitting the ball over the wall or missing it altogether.

I have never really understood the point of skiing. It costs a lot of money. You are cold and wet. You are tired. You get bruised. It is dangerous. You get up early in the morning to avoid the queues at the ski lifts but you never do. Everyone seems to get drunk every evening and thinks eating bread in hot cheese is the best thing ever. You then dance late into the night, have an hour's sleep, get up at the crack of dawn and queue in the freezing cold to do it all over again. No, I don't like skiing. Tom at four months was definitely too young to take ski lessons.

A trip to Vienna with Classic FM had been an altogether different, more civilised experience of Austria. It had been organised by the Austrian Tourist Board. They were promoting the food and wines of the region but there was also an opportunity to watch a performance of the Lipizzaner stallions at the Spanish Riding School in the Hofburg, and visit Piber, where the stallions are bred and kept.

The nearby city of Graz is famous for being Austria's former capital, and the birthplace of Arnold Schwarzenegger. I think they are more proud of Arnold than of anything else. It is a beautiful town and its cobbled streets and trams make it extremely picturesque. Arnold visits the place every year, once a year – presumably with the words 'I'll be back'.

On the trip to Vienna were a very interesting bunch of journalists including Brian Sewell, the art historian, who writes for the London *Evening Standard* and Pippa Cuckson, editor of another prestigious title, *Horse and Hound*. What Brian doesn't know about art isn't worth knowing and what Pippa doesn't know about horses I don't care to know.

Brian Sewell is the ideal person to take with you when you are walking around an art gallery. Any art gallery would do, but I think he was in his element at the Belvedere in Vienna. He speaks with a wonderful Noël Coward accent, and is not only extremely well read but has a wicked sense of fun. As we walked round the Belvedere he talked about the Dutch painters on display. I knew nothing about Dutch painters and up until then, I didn't really feel as though my life had been lacking as a result.

'People liked to collect these two painters in particular', he said, as he pointed at a painting. 'The cognoscenti had to be very discreet about collecting these paintings, Sarah. This artist was very much into depicting the seduction of minors and masturbation.'

(At this point I was wondering if my boss at Classic FM would allow the word 'masturbation' to be broadcast. When I had visited Guernsey the previous year someone had talked about Oliver Reed's penis – well, actually, about Oliver Reed's door knocker, which was supposedly shaped and moulded and about the same size as his penis. I could understand how that would appeal to the actor's sense of humour. Classic had allowed this, so why not a Dutch painter masturbating? Alastair, my boss at Classic, did allow it. He knew a good sound bite when he heard one. So to speak.)

The foals at Piber were very special. As Pippa Cuckson pointed out, 'Mares will not usually allow you to walk so close to their foals.' But these mares were different. Their large, dark brown eyes followed your every move but they allowed you even to touch their foals. 'They are very protective, but these horses have been brought up amongst humans, and they are at ease with them from the word go', Pippa said.

The Lipizzaners start out grey and turn white as they grow older. Apart from their big brown eyes, they have short, stout legs to support them when they jump into the air, and thickset bodies.

In my opinion – and I admit it is not a learned one – Lipizzaners do not look the most attractive of horses. They look squat and stubby but they glide and prance under the glass chandeliers of the Hofburg with grace and elegance, in the same way that seals may look ungainly on land but in their element in the water.

These animals are treated well. The antenatal ward in the Piber horse hospital was much better than the one in which I gave birth in Chelmsford. The expectant four-legged mums appear to be treated with much more care and reverence than a lot of two-legged ones.

****

So my memories of Austria were mixed. I couldn't decide whether to take Tom there in the summer or winter months. In the end we went in the spring.

We flew direct to Vienna with Austrian Airlines and it took just under two hours. The cabin crew were very efficient, good with Tom and good with me: friendly and very helpful. Vienna Airport (VIE – Wien-Schwechat) is 11 miles east of the city and as well as having restaurants, shops, bureaux de change, post office, bank and car hire outlets, it also has its own nursery. There is a regular bus service which takes you into the centre of town and to the major hotels.

When we arrived it was still very cold but the welcome at the hotel was warm and friendly. Tom was liked immediately and, thankfully, behaved impeccably. Although the receptionists were all smiles, I felt that if he had so much as sneezed or done anything other than sleep or smile sweetly, they would have been less friendly. In Italy, if Tom had screamed his little head off they would probably have laughed, picked him up and cooed in tune with his yells. I somehow got the impression that it wouldn't have been the same in Austria. Fortunately I never needed to find out as he behaved like a Stepford baby when we were there, with not a peep of bad temper. Everyone thought him an angel.

We visited the Belvedere again but this time without Brian Sewell – it wasn't quite the same. I had kept in touch with him since the trip and had told him I was expecting a baby. Eventually I let him know that I had had a little boy and that his name was Thomas. He had said, in his Noël Coward sort of way, 'what a lovely name', and then told me a very funny anecdote about Lady Gaitskell. Apparently she had told her fellow peers in the Wolfenden debate that 'if men gave birth to babies they wouldn't be so squeamish about sodomy'. I saw her point.

The Dutch paintings were still on display – the masturbators and the seducers of minors. Now I had a minor of my own, perhaps I found them rather less amusing. The baroque architecture, the palaces, the museums, the antique markets and shops of this glorious city were rather lost on Tom. He did have fun at Café Central, mushing up the sachertorte and being entranced by the string quartets that perform every afternoon. He bopped to Mozart and Strauss, Haydn and Brahms on my lap, as we people-watched. The Café Central is a wonderful place to do this and really child- and baby-friendly. Although smoking is allowed, and everyone seems to smoke in Vienna, there are areas which are smoke-free zones, and I was quickly shown to a table in one of them.

Smoking was a bit of a problem in Austria. There were some restaurants I didn't want to go into because of the smokers on each table. Generally I found on my travels that people seem to smoke more overseas than they do in England. Or perhaps it just felt that way now I was more alert to smoking's implications for Tom.

****

Out of town and away from the smokers, the city of Graz was still as fresh and charming as I remembered. The original hotel I had stayed in was still there, and that is where we stayed. It was full of ornate and antique furniture, which I knew, once Thomas could crawl, he would totally destroy. I'm sure even the cot they provided me with was a rare antique. It was fringed with silk lace and was made from mahogany. I almost didn't want to put Tom in it for fear he might damage it.

The next morning I took Tom to see the Lipizzaner stallions and walk amongst the foals. I explained why I was there and what I wanted to do, and we were allowed to make our visit.

I had produced a very positive report on Vienna and Graz for Classic FM. I think they remembered me as the mad reporter who had put microphones to the horses' mouths in the hope, perhaps, that one of them would say something. Preferably in English.

Walking once more through the horse maternity unit I realised how much time and care went into the breeding of these animals. I had watched them dance in the Spanish Riding School and I was impressed.

Tom, in turn, was fascinated by the snorting and put his fist up to their dark, wet nostrils. The horses didn't seem to mind. They let him touch their manes and giggle at them. The mares had such knowing, shiny brown eyes; they looked at me as if to say, 'Ah, you're a mother now too'.

LESSONS LEARNT IN AUSTRIA

1. Smoking
Always ask about smoking and non-smoking areas and rooms in hotels and restaurants. In my experience, people seem to smoke more in continental Europe than they do in the UK.

2. Stay cool and calm
Stay cool and calm, even when you feel yourself getting tense. The baby will know and react accordingly. If you are naturally a stressed-out sort of a person, I don't know how you will cope with being a mum let alone a travelling mum! Travel is very much about going with the flow and not letting the little – or the big – inconveniences get to you or your baby.

3. Ski resorts and babies
Ski resorts in both Europe and the States are excellent if you have a new baby. There are good crèches where babies are welcome from 12 weeks. Of course, you don't have to ski – you can enjoy the après ski – but it's a great way to get back into shape and have a first family holiday together if you have had a Christmas baby.

CANADA

Six Months

Of all the places I visit, I enjoy my time in Canada the most. I even loved Canada before I ever set foot on its soil. The place held a charm for me – the vastness of it all, the ultimate untamed wilderness. Its attractions include Arctic tundra, great wheatlands, and the Rocky Mountains as well as the Great Lakes, the St Lawrence River and Niagara Falls. I had heard that Canadians combine the sense of humour of the English with the enthusiasm for life and attitude to success of the Americans. To me this represented the best of both nationalities: the best of all worlds.

Of all the ten provinces and three territories in Canada, the Yukon is my favourite. It is a land of vast lakes, grizzly bears and glaciers.

There are more bald eagles there than in America (a fact no American mentions and every Canadian does). All nationalities seem to live there in genuine harmony and the First Nations – the native aborigines – are properly recognised for their role in the evolution of the country.

I travelled to Canada many times for Classic FM. My first trip was to Toronto – the third largest theatre capital in the world, as the Toronto press officer proudly announced on my arrival. As I then lived in the largest theatre capital in the world (London), I could not see why I should be attracted by the third largest. The press officer rather missed the point. Toronto has so many other selling points over and above its theatre – which is, admittedly, extremely good.

In my opinion, Canada's cities are not its unique selling point, although those I have visited (Vancouver, Toronto, Montreal, Quebec and Calgary) all have a distinct charm. Yes, they are cosmopolitan, have great night life and lots to do and see. The advertising also sells Canada as the Great Outdoors – and in that respect the pitch is right. Canada offers the definitive 'great outdoors'. Areas like Nova Scotia, Newfoundland and Prince Edward Island, Vancouver Island, and the prairie and wilderness towns of Winnipeg and Dawson City *are* unique selling points. These vast areas are unspoiled and untamed, and quite take one's breath away.

The Canadians seem to possess an innate respect for nature. The connection between those who live there and the land itself seems to be a spiritual one.

Some of the best reports I have ever done have come from commissions in Canada. I even won an award from the Canadian Tourism Commission for a report on Nova Scotia's annual music festival: The Celtic Colours on the island of Cape Breton.

When I was five months pregnant with Tom, I was asked to present a one-hour documentary on the Discovery Channel. This would involve following in the footsteps of the gold rush prospectors from Skagway, Alaska to Dawson City. (Actually, to be strictly truthful, I hadn't been asked – I'd beaten down doors to get the job. Such is the world of television.)

It would take the film crew two weeks to film, and I desperately wanted to be the presenter. But I was five months pregnant. Would the producers allow me to present a film which, by its very nature, needed someone who could climb mountains, ride in a helicopter over raging forest fires and vast glaciers, hunt for grizzlies, even ride white water? I had waited over ten years for this opportunity. I knew they were unlikely to take the risk. So I didn't tell them.

Of course, I was found out as soon as I arrived in Vancouver. The director's wife took one look at my eyes (ironically not a glance at my tummy, which was still small) and guessed. A woman's eyes change when she is pregnant. Did you know that? I didn't.

After some highly stressed international calls between me and the producer and the director and the executive producer, they eventually decided to keep me on, provided that I signed a letter saying that if anything happened to me or to Tom, it was my responsibility and not theirs. Thus began a journey more incredible than any I could ever have imagined.

We were to film in reverse order to the way the story was to be broadcast – starting at Dawson City, where most of the gold stampeders had ended their journey, and finishing in Skagway, Alaska where it had all begun.

This could prove difficult, as I would look increasingly less dishevelled and probably thinner as the programme progressed, when broadcast the right way round.

In Dawson City, the crew arranged for me to interview a number of locals. One evening, I dressed up as a showgirl in a big, red, frilly petticoat and strutted my stuff up on stage, complete with high kicks and the lot. The original showgirls provided a bit of frivolity in the harsh conditions in Dawson 100 years ago. And the showgirls of the 1990s still provided excellent entertainment for both locals and tourists.

Dawson City itself was not as I expected. The sidewalks may not have been paved with gold, but the people were a different matter. At the centenary celebrations, I met many of the descendants of those who had braved the journey all those years ago. They spoke with pride, with tears in their eyes, of their great grandparents who had risked life and limb in search of a fortune.

I also met a latter-day gold miner, Jerry Bride, who was mining land which had been mined three times before. He lived in a small shack just outside town and had fought off scurvy, grizzlies, frostbite, and severe malnutrition amongst other things during his time in Dawson. This man had more character in his little finger than most men have in their whole bodies. He lived alone. There had been a woman in his life, but she didn't like the life (it was too hard), so they had parted company. He showed me how to mine the land and identify the gold from the leaveright.

'Do you know what leaveright is, Sarah?' he asked.

'No. Another form of rock, I presume.'

'Well, the gold you pick up, right – and the leaveright – well you "leave it right" where it is. OK?'

Jerry was full of little quips like this. Several visitors had been inspired to write books about their journeys and Jerry always featured in their pages. It seems rude not to mention him in this one.

But Jerry wasn't the only character of note that I met in Dawson City. On an island about a fifteen-minute boat ride away I met Bessa. Bessa belongs to the First Nations; she is descended from one of the tribes who lived in Canada long before the settlers had claimed the land as their own. She was one of a group who welcomed visitors to an encampment called Ancient Voices.

The brochure described the place as a re-creation of an Indian village. I thought it would be a Disneyland version of the real thing, but it wasn't. It was really special.

Bessa led me through the surrounding forest area, telling me about the power of the plants, the flowers and the herbs: which were dangerous, which could be used medicinally, which were the natural Viagras of this world. The crew were particularly interested in the last of these. Bessa also showed me how air pollution gradually erodes the goodness in the soil, and how the same pollution destroys the trees. 'The trees are laughing and talking to you', she would say, as the wind rustled through their leaves.

After talking trees, we fished for wild salmon in the Yukon river. Once I had caught one, I had to learn in five minutes how to gut it, which Bessa showed me. For the camera, I had to learn, Blue Peter style, how to do something she had learnt from her mother as a child. Bessa was in her sixties when I met her.

I remember there being a lot of blood when I cut open the salmon, which the director liked, remarking that it looked like a scene from Carrie. I was using a knife the size of a machete, and could easily have sliced through my hand if I hadn't been careful.

I was told to cut the fish up into long strips so that it could be smoked in the wooden smoke-house in the corner of the encampment. The remainder we ate that night around a camp fire, while Bessa sang to us. She sang a haunting song and told me about the future Tom.

'He will be a healthy happy chap. He has been a long time in the coming. He has waited a long time.'

Bessa assured me everything would be fine. Someone made a rattle for 'Tom' out of sheep's horn and carved an image of an eagle on it, which would be his spiritual animal. It was just outside Dawson City, by that camp fire during Bessa's song, that 'Tom' first kicked.

****

So it was with absolute delight that I returned to Canada with Tom in tow. I had flown there so many times by myself, I wondered how different it would be this time.

Seven and a half hours to Toronto would be the longest flight Tom had taken to date. First we had to negotiate international departures. Tom had his passport now, and I wanted Canada to be the first stamp in it. We would be there for just over a week, staying at a hotel in central Toronto, which had nannies and babysitters available. We flew with Air Canada but with an economy ticket, so Tom would have to sit on my lap throughout. I guessed my legs would go numb.

As a 'mother with a young child', I was one of the passengers allowed on first. I had asked for a seat with maximum space and a cot. For a long haul flight, always book a cot, even if you think your baby won't sleep. Having room to stretch your legs if you have a baby on your lap for such a long time is also a necessity. Don't kid yourself it is a luxury.

Air Canada were brilliant. They had always been great when I travelled by myself, and they were just as good with the two of us.

Tom was proving to be an excellent flyer. He was, to be frank, totally disinterested. I thought he would be excited or at least a little winded by the take-off and landing. But no. He looked stony-faced at the window or smiled at the air hostess (he definitely has a soft spot for them.) and fell asleep within minutes of boarding the plane. He awoke to be fed and watered, and changed occasionally, but that was it.

Ah, changing a baby on a plane. Interesting scenario this one. There is not much room, even if you have a first- or business-class ticket. I had become an expert nappy-changer by this time – off and on, cleaned and moisturised, in under 60 seconds, dirty or not. But other passengers would look distinctly nervous when they saw me walking with Tom towards the toilet. I ignored them.

Mind you, I was grateful that I hadn't put on much weight when I was pregnant and therefore didn't have much to take off after he had been born. Manoeuvring yourself around a wash-room with a baby is difficult enough. If I had been on the plump side, it would have been nigh on impossible.

Changing a nappy on an aeroplane is a complete balancing act, where you need to co-ordinate the use of mouth, arms, hands, legs and feet.

Feeding Tom on the plane was made easier by the fact that he has an extremely healthy appetite. He will and does eat very well. I took my own organic baby food (Baby Organix). None of the airlines I have travelled with supply organic baby food; they do supply baby food, but it is not guaranteed GM-free. I was also still breastfeeding and could discreetly do so under my blouse or jumper as necessary.

For most of the journey Tom slept spread-eagled on top of me, his little seat belt attached by a loop to mine. I slept, or tried to sleep, at the same time. Fortunately, he was still quite small: a bigger or older baby would have been a real struggle.

We were met from the plane by a helpful courier who escorted us to collect the luggage and then to the taxi rank. Tom awoke. It was mid-morning and the place was buzzing. People were darting in and out of each other's way like busy bees, but very politely. They would just nod and smile and continue on their way.

The Lester B. Pearson Airport is a 20-minute drive from Toronto City. There is a regular bus service, but I took a taxi. The driver told me all about his six children, how he had lived in Toronto for six years, how he used to live in Montreal. One sentence followed another with hardly a breath in between. He went on to tell me how wonderful he thought Tom was, how worldly-wise he looked (at six months?), and how handsome, and that he would break women's hearts!

We were staying at the Royal York Hotel at 100 Front Street, opposite the train station – a venerable hotel if ever there was one, in fact one of the oldest in the city. It is within walking distance of the CN Tower, at the time the world's tallest free-standing structure, and also the Sky Dome, a multi-purpose entertainment complex and sports stadium which was the first building in the world to have a retractable roof. Tom looked up at the hotel as we drew near, craning his head for a good view. The Royal York is an extremely impressive old building in a very modern city, so it looks very slightly out of place.

The cab driver offered to carry all my luggage to my room, and Tom as well, to give me a break. The doorman almost had to prise the bags away from him, insisting that this was his job and what he was paid to do.

A smiling receptionist greeted me by name.

'Ms Tucker and Thomas Tucker, I presume.'

'Er, yes.' (I didn't want to go into the O'Reilly bit here, although Tom's passport had 'O'Reilly' on it.)

'We were expecting you at about this time. Welcome.'

I felt special already.

'We have prepared a room, please follow James', she said pointing to another smiling face. I followed James through several corridors to a lift.

Ah, lifts. Lifts are of course better than stairs, in that they save time and energy, but within them lie hidden dangers. Like revolving doors, they are a potential minefield for mothers with young babies. Don't, for example, take a buggy into a lift. You will take up room for three, unless it folds up small, and you will have the additional hassle of folding and unfolding it. In a lift designed for four, that means only room for yourself, your buggy and one other. But this doesn't stop other people getting into the lift with you. After all, it says four on the door, and the baby is only 'a bit' after all, not even a proper person.

I nickname these people 'the tutters'. The tutters are the martyrs in life, the 'woe is me' brigade. I have very strong feelings about them. You know them at first sight. They really come into their own in restaurants and hotels, in fact in any public place.

They don't say anything. They never complain aloud but have perfected a repertoire of sighs and tuts and looks which speaks volumes. They would make an Eskimo freeze.

There are a lot of tutters in England. In fact, I think tutting may be a purely English phenomenon. Consider other nationalities and how they complain. The Americans have turned complaining into an art form; they are the consummate professionals at making a lot of noise about anything they are not happy with. Not content with mere apology, they often sue if they can, and seem to get what they claim for. To the French and Spanish, complaining is a way of life and an excuse to exercise both the arms and the lungs. In the Far East, they never complain at all. To complain is a loss of face, it shows a weakness in character not a strength. In England, we sulk, we whine, we tut.

Fortunately there were no English (and no tutters) in the lift at the Royal York, which in any case was big enough for ten.

Our room overlooked the ornate railway station, which faces the hotel. There was a cot, large and wooden and welcoming, a baby changing station and a baby bath all ready in the en suite bathroom. In addition, the pack gave me a variety of baby-orientated information, such as where to find baby changing facilities, and people who were well-versed in baby care of all kinds. Basically all the questions you wanted to ask were answered. We were in safe hands at the Royal York Hotel.

I was very keen for Bessa to meet Tom. I wanted him to meet the lady who had sung to him before he was born. I contacted her and arranged to meet in the Yukon capital of Whitehorse. There are direct flights from Vancouver, and Dawson City would have been a long drive for Tom. By now he was an old pro at flying, airports and flirting with the cabin crew. He slept for most of the flight and consequently arrived at the small Whitehorse airport in brighter and breezier form than his mother.

Through the crowds at the busy terminal I heard a cry, 'Sarah, Sarah, is that you, Sarah?'

There, standing by the luggage conveyor, was not only Bessa, but the film crew I had worked with on the Discovery Channel project – Peter, Cliff and Randy, and the excellent public relations specialist, Lynda. It was so good to see them all and so unexpected that I burst into tears.

The visit was to be only a brief one, but we headed for a restaurant in the basement of one of the oldest hotels in the capital and sat for the next six hours, just chatting about everything and how well the documentary had done, how everyone was, and how alike Tom and I were.

Bessa sang to Tom again. We had emptied the restaurant by the end of our lunch, so there were no other diners to appreciate this unexpected floorshow. Her voice was so powerful, so strong, it filled the room like a heady perfume. Time stopped. I missed the backdrop of the valley at Ancient Voices and the 'laughing' trees, of course, but it didn't matter. Tom loved it. He even clapped.

LESSONS LEARNT IN CANADA

1. Space on long haul flights

Book a cot well in advance if you are flying long haul. This will give you space as well as your baby. When ringing to confirm the cot, take a name and preferably get confirmation in writing from the airline that you have requested one.

2. Food on flights

Most airlines offer baby food, but check in advance. When I contacted Emirates, for example, they told me that they offer organic baby food on request if specified. However, I recommend that you always take your own, especially on a long haul flight. It is not a good idea to try out anything 'new' on your baby's tummy on a long flight. If you are still feeding him yourself, all the better.

3. Lifts and revolving doors

You'll encounter these in most large hotels. It will say room for x number of people. If you have a baby and a buggy, count yourself as three just to be on the safe side. Also mind your baby's hands and toes in lift doors and revolving doors. Babies can and do stick them out at the most inconvenient times and the most incredible angles.

HONG KONG

Seven Months

Hong Kong inspired my spirit and thirst for adventure. I felt more at home there than I did in England; more relaxed and content.

The first time I travelled to Hong Kong I was 21, and went to visit my cousin and her family who lived in Stanley on Hong Kong Island. Her husband worked for Barclays International. The family travelled all over the world and had settled in well to the expatriate luxury lifestyle. With maids and butlers and chauffeurs and nannies, they went out to dinner each evening. Sports clubs filled the days of the ladies who shopped till they dropped. They made the Knightsbridge ladies-who-lunch look like amateurs.

My cousin, however, is practical and grounded and wanted to fill her days and head with more than shopping. I was invited to stay with them for two weeks. I was only able to go because my cousin had kindly offered to put me up (or put up with me – depending on which way you look at it).

This trip to Hong Kong was my first journey overseas without a chaperone. I loved travelling by myself.

The flight into the island was breathtaking. We seemed to fly between the flats and saw the women hanging out the washing from their windows and cooking lunch in their kitchens. You could almost see the whites of their eyes.

The Hong Kong lifestyle is one big rollercoaster from the word go. From the minute you land, the pace of the place takes your breath away and you feel lost in its energy, colour and noise. It assaults all the senses. It was totally different to anything I had ever experienced before. People didn't talk. They seemed to shout at one another. They weren't scared to be heard.

The very old and the very young were treated with care and consideration in the streets. They seemed to gain energy from the crowd – unlike in England where old people walk with a hesitant gait, these little old men and women bustled their way through as though they were thirty years younger.

The markets sell fascinating things like hundred-year-old eggs and bird's nest soup and dried bat's wing. This was all so weird and wonderful to me. I even tried to get a job out there, albeit half-heartedly.

The American navy were in town, many of them Tom Cruise look-a-likes, I kid you not. I went on a one-day excursion to the Sung Dynasty Village (a re-creation of a thousand-year-old Chinese village) and some of the 'boys' were on the trip. A middle-aged Scottish woman was also by herself on the trip and befriended me. She chatted up some of the sailors and they invited us both – much to my horror – back to the bar in their barracks. They were, we were told, the elite of the crew, the Top Guns.

We arranged to meet them at a certain time in a certain bar. One, who looked a lot like Tom Cruise (perhaps his brother) asked me if I would like to go out to dinner with him. I thought I knew what this really meant, but I wasn't sure. So I chose instead to take the safe option and meet two girls who were the daughters of a friend of my cousin's. They were my age but a hundred per cent more street wise, which wasn't difficult in those days.

We had supper in a Mongolian restaurant where you help yourself to various bits of chicken and fish and vegetables and someone cooks it for you. Every ten minutes I would look at my watch to see how close I was to meeting the Tom Cruise look-a-like. I imagined myself saying to the other two girls, 'I have to go now, I'm meeting someone'. But I didn't have the guts. The time came and went, and I comforted myself by thinking that probably he hadn't turned up either.

One of the two girls had just broken up with her boyfriend and wanted to win him back by getting a butterfly tattooed on to her left buttock. We went to the red light district of Wan Chai, up a narrow stairway to a little room where the walls were covered with different tattoo designs: dragons and insects and tigers and devils, and things which looked much better on a wall than they would on a body.

The girl who was having the tattoo done was by now very drunk. We had been to six pubs before ending up at the tattoo joint and by this time she was swaying to imaginary music. She kept asking if she was doing the right thing, but totally ignored our advice when we said 'No'. A seedy-looking man asked her to lift her skirt so that he could survey the canvas on which he had to work. 'Where you like it, missy?' 'There.' The girl prodded her cheek. 'This one.'

I didn't look. The man turned a machine on which started to zzzzzz and we sat patiently in the corner, looking at what the girl could have had other than the blue and pink butterfly she had chosen.

There was the sound of laughter in the hallway and in marched about a dozen American naval officers, all wanting tattoos on their backs. Big black ugly ones – no dainty butterflies for them. No, they preferred Napalm Death in big black letters with devil's horns, or a naked woman in a sports car, or something deep and meaningful like a girl's name and a woman's face crying.

The butterfly finished, we made our way to a night club. One of the Tom Cruise look-a-like's friends was there. Apparently he had waited for me after all, for over an hour. A missed opportunity or a lucky escape? I'll never know.

A day later, on the plane home from Hong Kong, I cried. I really regretted leaving a place that had almost literally swept me off my feet. For two weeks I had been without parents, been myself, by myself.

The next time I went to Hong Kong was with Tom's father, more than ten years later. We returned to Wan Chai, Hong Kong's entertainment centre and red light district once more. We went with friends to one of those girly bars where they do interesting things with poles and snakes and darts and ping-pong balls, contorting their bodies into interesting positions. I can never watch table tennis with a straight face these days.

When Tom and I went, we stayed at my cousin's apartment. She had a new husband (having divorced Barclay's man, who was back in England) and a new apartment. She had literally gone up in the world as she was now living on The Peak, the social and geographical peak of Hong Kong Island. Her apartment had brilliant views over the island and beyond.

Tom was as excited as I was by this particular trip. We flew into Hong Kong, this time not through the buildings but over the sea. Since my last visit, Hong Kong International Airport had been rebuilt, Kai Tak airport being replaced by Chek Lap Kok. Our arrival was less dramatic, but the airport building itself is incredible.

Designed by British architect Sir Norman Foster, the airport terminal is the largest single building in Hong Kong and its wing-like roof and glass walls have been hailed as a landmark in modern architecture. According to the literature, threequarters of the land used to rebuild the airport terminal had been reclaimed from the sea. As airport terminals go, it was stunning.

The world's largest suspension bridge (1.4 miles of it) – the Tsing Ma Bridge – had also been built since my last visit. This links Hong Kong to the island of Lantau, with its luxury resort and country club.

My cousin was there to greet us. Tom was bubbling with excitement but a bit overwhelmed by the noise. Everyone was shouting, even the children, so Tom thought he would shout as well.

There are bus, rail and taxi links from the airport to central Hong Kong which is about 28 miles away. But probably the quickest route is via the Airport Express Line, an all-seater, business-class high speed train which runs daily between 6am and 1am. It leaves every 8 minutes and takes 23 minutes to reach central Hong Kong.

However, we drove, with my cousin. She told me Hong Kong had changed considerably since it had been returned to Chinese ownership, but that it was still an interesting place to live and she would be sad to leave, which she eventually had to do at the end of the year. Each night, we sat in her Peak apartment, just looking at the view as though it was some huge television screen showing a must-see blockbuster feature. It was our own little panorama on the world.

Tom enjoyed the shopping excursions to Stanley Market in a little village on the coast, and to the night market in Temple Street in

Kowloon. He loved the large, glitzy shopping centres; and the shiny clean MTR (mass transit railway), Hong Kong's equivalent to the London Underground. For HK$70 you can travel all over Hong Kong for the week. The system runs to time, is clean and efficient and has only one drawback, which I noticed as I was with Tom. The seats are metallic, and, as the train stops and starts, passengers not in the know go sliding from one side of the carriage to the other. If you are by yourself this is amusing. If you are with a baby, it is a real hazard. Obviously, it helps if you are packed in like sardines as at least you don't fall over.

If you are travelling with a baby, everyone is considerate: they immediately stand up for you and there is no question of declining their offer. If someone offers you a seat, youaccept it wherever you are. End of story. Even the expatriates know that. It is frowned upon not to treat the very young and old with respect.

The women selling their wares in Temple Street chatted to Tom non-stop – as though he would understand them. He looked as though he did because he seemed to nod in all the right places.

On one occasion, while shopping in Kowloon, we visited a small dusty old shop selling antique boxes; it looked like a Dickensian curiosity shop. An old man came to serve us. Were we interested in anything? Had we been in Hong Kong long? Had I visited before, he wanted to know. He looked at me and then at Tom, and asked if he could hold him. A little hesitantly I agreed. Very gently he took Tom from my arms and held him in front of his nose. Then he swung him up in the air until they were nose to nose, then down again, looking straight into Tom's big blue eyes, all the time.

'This one here. This one has been here before. Old spirit. Very old spirit. He been here before. He at home here.' Then he looked at me. 'His mum at home here too.'

LESSONS LEARNT IN HONG KONG

1. Staying with relatives

If you can stay with friends or relatives while travelling, it's a good idea. They should know the place and be able to offer an insider's guide as to what to see, how to make best use of your time and, most important, what to avoid.

2. Food-warming

Babies shouldn't get used to having everything warmed up for them. They can drink cold milk, they can eat cold food. They only start to get fussy if you let them. Milk-warming or food-warming facilities may not always be available – but you won't need them if your baby doesn't mind.

3. Selfish space

Be aware of the space that you are occupying. Lots of women become very selfish when they have babies – especially when they take their baby around in a buggy. They can take up a lot of room – other people's room. In the first year most babies are light enough to carry in a front carrier, so be considerate, use one whenever possible.

AUSTRALIA

Seven Months

Australia is the largest island in the world or the smallest continent, depending on which way you look at it. It is almost the same size as the mainland of the United States of America, spans three time zones, has some of the driest areas on earth and enormous snowfields the size of Switzerland.

The first time I visited Australia, I was on a press trip, again working for Classic FM. I was there by default as another journalist had dropped out at the last minute. The group included reporters from the broadsheets, the tabloids, from radio and from some of the men's magazines.

The flight is a long one. It took more than 24 hours via Los Angeles on Air New Zealand. The airline looked after us brilliantly: I couldn't

and can't fault them. I sat in first-class next to the public relations manager, which I had been dreading.

The thought of 24 hours non-stop hard sell from a double-barrelled Sloaney Ab-Fab PR was depressing. I geared myself for a long stint of hype, puff and fluff.

I was wrong. This PR person was different. She was a laugh, she had a great sense of humour and I liked her. I wanted to stay awake so that I could chat to her some more. She became and still is a very good friend.

We saw little of either Los Angeles (because it was dark as we flew in and we weren't allowed out of the airport), or Sydney, our arrival point in Australia, because it was cloudy. Also we had to catch a connecting flight to Adelaide, South Australia's state capital and by far its most populated town. From there we flew direct to the Flinders Ranges, a region of granite peaks and spectacular and colourful gorges, dotted with eucalyptus trees. Our group had been invited to Australia ostensibly to attend the 'Opera in the Outback' concert, a performance by Dame Kiri Te Kanawa, but I was more interested in visiting the wine-growing areas of the Clare and Barossa Valleys. South Australia produces over half of all Australian wine and some of its best.

The Flinders Ranges are not really the outback, more the gateway to it. The dawn chorus at Arkaroola, at the northern peak, was incredible, providing the most wonderful alarm call you could imagine. The dramatic, exhilarating scenery, with kangaroos bouncing about all over the place, added to an unforgettable experience.

Next, we flew on to Parachilna where we stayed in a luxury tent encampment. Well, it was supposed to be a luxury tent encampment. It actually consisted of 200 or so small ridge tents offering the basics and little else. There was one hotel in Parachilna but it was full.

The Dame Kiri concert was due to take place at nearby Yalkarinha. But first we visited a resort called Wilpena Pound, right in the centre of the Flinders Ranges, to listen to a string quartet play Vivaldi's Four Seasons.

Amongst the eucalyptus, a romance was blossoming. The photographer had his eye on a journalist from a small press group from the States which had joined us. It was probably to be expected, with all this fresh air, Vivaldi and pent-up energy. Occasionally these things happen on press trips but not as often as people think.

Sometimes people just click. There we were on the other side of the world, with no inhibitions and no one at home to know unless someone sneaked.

I was always too busy with the microphone to worry about what I looked like or what anyone else looked like for that matter. But I have always been fascinated watching others interact.

The photographer sat alone under a tree, all moody and brooding, smoking his fortieth cigarette of the day. 'I smoke the equivalent of only seven full-fat cigarettes a day with these ultra-low ones' he would say if anyone suggested there might be a health risk. The American journalist went over to sit with him. He was, after all, a male on his own, and seemed to know a lot about Australia. So obviously she went over to ask him some questions.

The next day we were due to interview Dame Kiri after a visit to the annual Beltana picnic races. Everyone from the outback seems to congregate in that one area for the day and race anything – pigs, goats, cows, ferrets, camels – and, of course, horses. It's fun, incredibly noisy and very Australian. Beltana's one claim to fame, other than the annual races, is that it is the first place in Australia to have a camel breeding farm.

Everyone lets their hair down and screams at the top of their voices when the animals reach the finishing line. The horses have names like Will He, Won't He; Almost There; and Better Luck Next Time. So, as you may expect, sometimes they don't make it to the finish line. They just stop mid-track and nibble at a bit of stray grass. It's not exactly Ascot.

At the pre-arranged press conference that afternoon we interviewed Dame Kiri, who was enchanting and helpful and gave us some good soundbites. The night of the concert, we were supposed to wear black tie and long dresses. We didn't. It was cold and the group dressed for the climate not the occasion. Four layers of thermals and a jumper.

The concert itself was magnificent. The New Zealand diva sang a mixture of opera and contemporary music, including songs from Cats and West Side Story. There wasn't a dry eye in the outback. When all the clapping had died down and the last encore had been sung, we walked back to our base and had a drink at one of the makeshift bars which had been built to cater for the tent encampment at Parachilna. As we all said goodnight, I noticed the photographer and the journalist stayed behind. I went back to my tent and very quickly fell asleep.

The bed, though basic, was very comfortable. I was determined not to dream about spiders or snakes or any of the things we were told were common in this part of Australia.

It must have been only a few hours later when I awoke to a very loud and prolonged groaning noise. At first, I thought it was an animal: perhaps a dingo having a fight. But it sounded very close, almost as if it was in the tent next to me. It was.

I heard the noise again. No, that wasn't an animal, it was somebody groaning. With pleasure. Very loudly.

Where was my tape recorder? Where was my tape recorder? Why could I never find it when I needed the bloody thing? Where did I leave it? I was groping about in the dark. I wasn't the only one.

I heard an American voice which I recognised.

'No, I said no. No. I said no.'

The photographer obviously didn't understand no.

'No ... Well, all right then.'

She obviously didn't mean no.

Eventually they fell asleep, and so did I.

Next morning I was tired. The bed had not been that comfortable after all and my back ached. Everyone from the encampment was up and about early as the concerts had finished and people wanted to get back to the relative comfort of their own beds.

There was no sign of the photographer or the journalist, but the photographer's equipment – camera, lenses, film – which must have cost thousands of pounds, was on the table outside his tent, where it had obviously been all night.

We all left our tents to get breakfast. It had been organised by local students and was a brilliant affair: there was fresh fruit, bacon, eggs of all descriptions, tomatoes, mushrooms, and many different types of bread and cereal. Wonderful. The fresh air gave everyone a healthy appetite.

There was no sign of the journalist. I could have been cruel and asked the photographer if he'd seen her, but I didn't. As I returned to my tent to pack, I knew he was grinning from ear to ear behind my back.

Later that day we all drove to Thorn Park Country House in the Clare Valley, one of the foremost wine-growing regions in the state. Thorn Park is an 1850s homestead hotel, with six bedrooms, complete with verandahs, four-poster beds and shelves full of old books in every room. David Hay (the chef) and Michael Speers own this little idyll in the middle of 50 acres of parkland, which looks very English apart from the gum trees.

The journey by road to Thorn Park had been long but the reception we received was warm and welcoming and the food David prepared was glorious. The journalist and photographer studiously avoided looking at each other and sat at opposite ends of the table.

From the Clare Valley we drove on to the Barossa Valley, which is just 34 miles from Adelaide. Originally a settlement of German refugees in the 1830s, the area is notable for its Lutheran churches, good restaurants and fine vineyards. We gave the churches a miss but headed for the restaurants and vineyards where tastings and tours can be easily arranged – especially if you're a group of journalists from England or the States

The first stop was St Halletts. We toured the vineyard, sampled some of the wine and I tried to record the 'sound of the vines'. They made none – but at least I tried. Then we visited Peter Lehmann, who opened his home and heart to the group. At lunch he told us how the community works together, supporting local artists, by using their illustrations on wine labels and showing their work on the wine tours. Classical and jazz concerts are held regularly in the wine cellars and even amongst the vines during the summer. His enthusiasm was heady stuff, even without the fine wines we were being offered.

****

The photographer and the journalist weren't the only ones who had a romance on that trip. I had fallen for South Australia, or what I had seen of it, in a big way. The people have such a lust for life. They seem to be so positive. They work and play very hard and have the best food and wine – and attitude – that I had found anywhere on my travels. So when I returned to Australia with Tom, I had very high expectations.

This time round, there would be no Dame Kiri, no string quartet, no open house from Peter Lehmann or Michael and David at Thorn Park. This time the focus of attention was Tom.

Always, always, always prepare well in advance for long haul flights. If you don't you will spend your time at your destination recovering and dreading the flight back.

Tom invariably woke up when food was served, so I always ordered a fruit plate – no fiddly knives and forks, and also I was usually served before anyone else. If I had to, I could eat and play with Tom at the same time.

If you have successfully nagged your way into a seat with a bit of extra space, or where there is a pull-out cot, then you will find travelling long haul much more pleasurable.

In my experience, long haul carriers are much better equipped for mothers with young babies than short haul ones. An unhappy baby for 12 hours plus is obviously more of a problem than an unhappy baby for a few hours. British Airways, Cathay Pacific, Air New Zealand, Qantas, Virgin, Singapore Airlines, and especially Emirates, are all very good with babies. They take care of both mother and baby and make you feel human and special. I found it a pleasure, not a battle, travelling with them.

My inaugural journey to Oz with Tom was tolerable and he made lots of new friends, smiled and giggled and picked up an Australian twang to add to his growing vocabulary of goos and ahhhhs. We arrived on time at Sydney airport, which is large and clean and efficient. The baby-changing facilities are good and relatively easy to find.

I had visited Australia once more before this trip, when I had been invited to cover the Gay Mardi Gras in Sydney. Once a year, the city is taken over by a festival of the most colourful and exotic proportions. On Mardi Gras night everyone is positively euphoric, not simply glad to be gay. In my view this was an event strictly for adults, so I decided not to take Tom to Sydney when the Mardi Gras was in full swing. I'm sure he would have enjoyed looking at the pretty girls: even though most of them were boys.

Sydney did not meet my expectations I'm afraid. It may be the largest natural harbour in the world but I was disappointed. To be fair, my expectations were extremely high. Sydney is sold that way: wonderful beaches, outdoor lifestyle, youth and sunshine and sand.

I had expected it to be incredibly beautiful and trendy and exotic. Perhaps I didn't give the place enough time – after all, I stayed there for only a long weekend on each occasion – but I was still disappointed.

First of all, it's not the sort of place you can easily walk around on foot as you can with most cities, even in London. There are trains and buses and even a monorail. When I was there as a reporter, I went on the back of a Harley Davidson to visit the beaches and leafy suburbs, which was fantastic and an ideal way to see the place. Great if you're single, but hardly practical with a baby.

Sydney is quite hilly. You notice this even more when you have a baby wrapped around you. The beaches are great and plentiful, some more trendy and crowded than others, but I didn't see many babies or young children playing on them. Mostly it was just young hippy chicks and guys surfing or just wearing the surfing gear. You can take boat trips out into the harbour but these seem mainly for the beautiful youth, not wrinkly oldies or a pushchair Pom.

Everything in Sydney seems to be aimed at entertaining the young and fit and energetic, but this leaves both the old and the very young rather in limbo. There are lots of bars and clubs catering for the young and young at heart, plus fashion shops, boutiques, and restaurants. There didn't seem to be many places that catered for children or babies. Didn't people have them in Sydney?

Certainly, I didn't notice many people with young children on my first visit. But then I wouldn't, would I? It's not until you have one yourself that you tend to notice others.

It is the same with pregnancy. You only take in that other women are pregnant when you are yourself. Perhaps this is mother nature helping you to realise that you are not alone.

Sydney's youth fest didn't matter when I was there by myself, but obviously it did when I was with Tom. The fact that the lifts in the little boutique hotels were ridiculously small, and that there was a lot of noise from the neighbouring streets while we tried to sleep, now mattered quite a lot.

In Adelaide and the Barossa Valley it was different. Adelaide is much smaller and much more compact than Sydney. It is easy to find your way around and easy to walk there. I did see mothers with their children in the streets and it seemed much more of a community and less of a cosmopolitan metropolis.

Adelaide's parks and museums welcomed mothers with babies, and the hotels offered cots and special services (such as rooms on lower floors, by the lifts) for them. It was a friendlier, slower place and no less attractive or uninteresting for that.

Half an hour's drive away from Adelaide, in the Barossa Valley, I went to visit David and Michael and show them Tom. I doubted they would remember me, but they did, and they were really sweet with Tom. They sat him in the middle of one of the many large round tables in their restaurant and offered to make him some wonderful concoction with fresh ingredients, well mushed up so that he could eat it. He did and loved it. I was delighted with the adult version.

The harpist who entertains the guests even played Humpty Dumpty for him – not an easy task I should imagine – and Away in a Manger, which I had sung (albeit very badly) to Tom since his birth on 20 December seven months earlier.

We stayed in one of the six rooms. Tom loved his little cot and I had a four-poster bed all to myself. The view from the window was like something one might see in Ireland. The fields were green and lush and the air sweet. I had always thought of Australia as being an outback of wasteland with little else before I visited the Barossa.

Ah, the outback. Would I return to it, or at least its gateway, with Tom? I wanted him to see the kangaroos.

But then I remembered the tale of the baby being eaten by a dingo, and I wondered if it would be the wisest thing to do. And after all, Parachilna wasn't really in the outback, any more than the Flinders Ranges were. I decided to leave such a visit at least until Tom was a toddler. That might be a different book: Have Toddler Will Travel.

LESSONS LEARNT IN AUSTRALIA

1. City guides

Some cities cater for mothers with babies better than others. In general, the more cosmopolitan and fast the city, the less likely it is to be suitable for a mother with a baby, albeit a young one in a front carrier. Consult the guide books which can and do help. If you have access to the internet, some of the best information is contained in Columbus Travel Guides, which are also available in hard copy. Website address is www.wtg-online.com. Dorling Kindersley's guides and especially Insight Guides are also great visually and very user friendly although not 'mother and baby' specific.

NEW ZEALAND

Seven Months

I had only ever visited New Zealand once before taking Tom there. It seemed an awfully long way to take a baby (28 hours from London to Auckland) to prove a point. But I was determined to retrace all my steps.

I had learnt from flying to Australia that long haul economy seats do offer more than short haul, especially if you ask for a cot as you will get more space in front of you anyway. Obviously if you can get an upgrade, so much the better – although other passengers may not agree.

At a recent press launch the issue of travelling with a baby in first or business class was discussed. A journalist friend admitted that after one business class flight he had actually written to the airline to complain about the noise from a mother with two young children but

had heard nothing from them. I nearly told him that he was a pompous, selfish twit but I also sympathised with him. Pre-Tom I would have been exactly the same, and probably even more objectionable. I might even have complained during the flight itself.

The journalist's argument was that he had paid extra for his seat to get some peace and to have more room. He could sleep or work surrounded by like-minded people who would respect his need for quiet. He understood that some companies pay for expatriate families to travel business class, and that they should take advantage of this when travelling with their children. My cousin, for example, when she was with Barclays International, always travelled with her children in first class and probably drove other passengers mad: but the quality of her journey was much improved.

The whole issue is a difficult one. Do you refuse to take someone with their baby in first or business class, when they are able to pay for it? If an adult was as rowdy as some babies are when flying, they would be handcuffed to the seat and arrested for air rage. But babies can scream and bash the seats about and it can all be blamed on teething.

Currently, none of the airlines will refuse to take your baby first or business class. The only way they can deal with unhappy babies is for the crew to become proficient in baby care. Interestingly, you will find that most crew who serve first and business class passengers are fully trained in nursery care. This does make you wonder if this is for the benefit of babies or for adults who behave like babies.

****

All airline services sound good on paper. Only experiencing them first hand and putting them to the test can you really make a sound judgement. According to my experience, Air New Zealand was a very good way to fly.

The first time I travelled to New Zealand I found it a rather surreal experience. Looking out of the window as you fly into Auckland, you think that someone has played a trick on you. It looks as though you are flying over the fields of Devon. Everywhere is lush and green and it looks just like the West Country. When I left the plane, I wanted to kiss the ground: I was on the other side of the world. It felt very strange indeed.

I had arrived at a peculiar time, because the lights had literally gone out in Auckland. There had been a huge power cut which had cut all the electricity into the city and it would be weeks, even months, before the lights were fully on again. The Australian press was full of jokes at the New Zealanders' expense, such as 'last one out please remember to turn the light off' and that sort of thing, but worse.

It is a common misconception that the two countries are just a stone's throw from each other, a bit like popping over to France for the weekend from the UK. In fact, the flight from Sydney to Auckland takes 3 hours 30 minutes. That is no hop, skip and jump.

The South Island of New Zealand has a temperate climate very similar to that of England, while in the North it is subtropical. The South can be quite cool, with snow in the mountains but the North has no extremes of heat or cold. While the east often experiences drought, the west generally has more rain.

In the South Island, places like Dunedin and Invercargill in the Otago region have strong Scottish roots (Dunedin even has a 'Scottish Week' in March). On the edge of the Canterbury Plains lies the 'Garden City' of Christchurch, the South Island's largest city, and a very English one, like a university town.

On our flight to New Zealand Tom was great. Even the businessmen thought so. Admittedly they did look at us when we first entered as if to say 'what the hell are you doing in the business class section' but Tom remained quiet and didn't even whimper. I fed him discreetly during the flight without fuss or raised eyebrows.

The lights were on this time when we landed in Auckland. Tom had slept for much of the flight, yet seemed tired and dehydrated, which is bad for adults but dangerous for babies. I therefore spent a few hours in the nursing rooms at Auckland airport just nursing Tom. He was very quiet and so was I. The room which had been provided was very clean and bright and a very pleasant start to our time on the other side of the world.

The flight on to Wellington, New Zealand's capital, would take about an hour. We had about four hours to wait before our flight into the windy city. Windy Wellington certainly is windy. Even windier than Chelmsford.

Wellington lies on a steep hillside overlooking a deep harbour. It is the country's centre of nightlife, arts, culture, fashion and restaurants. On my first visit to Wellington, I had been to the Te Papa Museum, which had just been opened that month, on the waterfront. I remember making my way to the building, and nearly being blown off my feet. This time I made sure that I held on to Tom tightly when I went out. It is very exposed to the sea is Wellington and the wind whips into the town as though to give it a regular spring clean every hour on the hour throughout the day.

On my first visit I had stayed in a self-catering apartment in the centre of town. It was clean, modern, almost luxurious and spacious with excellent views – almost penthouse potential. I decided to stay there again and see how things compared when baby came too. There was a cot, baby food in the mini-bar, and bottles and sterilising equipment if you wanted it. As well as the nuts and crisps and health bars, there were disposable nappies, baby wipes and nappy sacks. Marvellous. The best thing was that the nappies were the right size for Tom. I had been asked how old he was and they had chosen exactly the right size.

I decided to take Tom to Te Papa. The museum had impressed me on my first visit and I wanted to see if it was as good or even better the second time round. The exhibits are a celebration of New Zealand's history and culture. They are well set out and completely fascinating. And I don't particularly like museums.

Te Papa covers the time right from the arrival of the early settlers, who were fishermen, demonstrating the importance of whale fishing in New Zealand's development. Part of the exhibition I saw consisted of a ballet based on the relationship between the whale and the fisherman. It was very powerful, with much Maori singing. At the end of the performance there was ironic mockery of the false pretensions of the New Age generation wanting the singing of whales to induce sleep in the young and harmony in the world: such pretentious twaddle. I wanted to see what Tom would make of the whale sounds and the Maori singing, which tends to make most people sit up and think. He slept through the whole performance.

At this museum you could also try your hand at a simulated bungee jump. I personally think this is a waste of time. If you want to scare yourself to death, why not do it for real in Queenstown where the sport began just over ten years ago? But there were queues of people wanting to take part, and those who had tried the simulator left with wide, manic grins on their faces. Those in the queue also had wide, manic grins on their faces. They all looked quite mad.

I headed to Queenstown next, as I had done on my original visit.

Queenstown has everything for everyone. It is a major centre for ski enthusiasts from all over the world. It is situated by Lake Wakatipu at the foot of the Remarkables mountain range. (You can imagine, the local PR and advertising companies have a field day with that name. Everything about Queenstown is 'remarkable'.) The town provides excellent hiking in national parks which cover over five million acres. The scenery includes forests, thermal areas, valleys, glaciers, coastal bays and mountains. Ornithologists flock here (excuse the pun) to watch the varied bird life and the area is also a haven for rare ferns and heathers. The Abel Tasman Park, one of New Zealand's three coastal parks, can be reached by foot or by boat from Kaiteriteri, which is how I had travelled there on my first trip to Queenstown.

Then, I had gone to Queenstown to scare myself witless by bungee jumping off a hundred-year-old bridge, aerobatic flying, paragliding loop the loops, jet boating, and many other things which would frighten most people into submission. I did it all for the sake of getting a good radio report.

The first stop was the bungee jump. I interviewed the guy who showed me the ropes, literally and metaphorically. 'It's made out of the same material as condoms – so it's perfectly safe.' (Oh yeah?)

'People over 60 are allowed to go for free.'

'Really? Do you have many takers?'

Oh, yes, we have coachloads!'

There didn't seem to be any there on the day I went.

'Would you like to have a go?'

'Yes. Could I record while I'm doing it?'

'Sure, but you won't be able to hold the mike. We'll hold it for you and record you screaming as you drop down. OK?'

'OK.'

I described into the microphone how they weighed me, writing my weight on my wrist so that the length of the rope was right. I probably sweated off a few pounds just waiting.

'Would you like a video of this?'

'Why not, rude not to.' Something I could show my children I thought at the time. Nutter.

He tied a towel around my ankles and a rope around the towel and made me hobble to the end of the bridge. I described what he was doing into the microphone and all the time was thinking to myself

'This will make good radio. This will make good radio. I sound really nervous. Fear sounds good. People will empathise with me.'

As I stood at the edge of the hundred-year-old wooden bridge looking out to nowhere, I really couldn't give a damn about anyone empathising with me. I didn't care if anyone ever empathised with me again. I now knew I was completely nuts. I had gathered an audience. A female Pommy – a *journalist* female Pommy no less – was about to jump. Would she have the balls to do it? I had an audience now – I couldn't chicken out.

'Just look straight ahead and jump Sarah. Count to three'.

'One.'

'Two.'

'Three.'

I jumped. I didn't hesitate for one minute. Not for a second. I knew if I did I wouldn't do it. Just like most things in life. So I jumped blind into the unknown, putting my trust in a piece of rope which had held hundreds of others, both heavier and lighter, but which might, just might, break under my weight.

The unexpected thing about bungee jumping is not that you go up and down: you expect that. But you don't expect to spin like a top. Some people knock themselves out with their own hands as they spin up and down uncontrollably. Not everyone spins it I'm told, but I did. Another unexpected thing is that there is no sudden jolt as you reach the bottom. You just curve up and down as though on a great big giant rubber band. I would never, ever do it again even if someone paid me a lot of money or paid Tom a lot of money. I was later told that you can detach a retina by bungee jumping. Well, my eyesight, touch wood, is still OK, but I haven't had the courage to watch the video.

As well as bungee jumping, jet boating (which entailed being driven at speed at the side of canyons and just missing), and paragliding (climbing to the top of a hill and jumping into nothingness supported by a guide and a pair of canvas wings) I also took a trip in an aerobatic plane. The pilot was very sweet and patient with me. I told him that I had already been jet boating and bungee jumping and paragliding that day, so I was a bit dizzy.

'Ah, then this will be a piece of piss, dear.'

'Do you get only macho types doing this sort of thing?' I asked hesitantly.

'Oh no, every type. In fact the best ones are the little old Japanese ladies who want to have a thrill. I take them in the plane and think I've got to be gentle and all they want to do is loop the loop and dead falls, and fly upside down for ages, and stall. When we land, they always come up smiling and laughing and giggling. You'd think they have been on a family outing or something. I call them the kamikaze clique.

'The worst are the Americans who think they can do anything, the big ones who only just fit in the cockpit. I had one guy, I think he was from Texas, who was really full of it. Been there, done that, seen everything. Well, I thought I'd be gentle, so we did a few loop the loops and an upside down and I noticed he was very quiet. Not shouting or laughing or anything any more. So I cut the trip short. When we landed he got out and threw up in his shoe. Just shows you. You can't judge anyone by appearances.'

He looked me up and down. I don't know if I looked the part – probably just looked like a dizzy blonde. Which I was. Dizzy, that is, not blonde.

'Right, well, I can't interview you while I'm up there so I'll interview you when we land.'

I got in the cockpit and put on my helmet and he showed me how to strap myself in. I thought the straps looked very insubstantial and asked if anyone had fallen out. I was told only a few times. He said this with a smile. I smiled back.

The plane made an awful lot of noise, but we quickly ascended into the sky, and flew over Queenstown and the surrounding glorious countryside. Queenstown was such a beautiful area, I wondered why anyone would want to nearly kill themselves in an Eden like this. It seemed so unnecessary. Then we started: loop the loop, upside down, dead fall, twists and turns. The sky became the land and land the sky.

I closed my eyes. I thought if I did this it would be just like a rollercoaster and not be so scary. It wasn't. But after a few minutes I felt a tapping on my helmet. I opened my eyes.

'You've got your eyes closed. You've got your eyes closed! Open them – you're cheating!'

I spent the next 10 minutes screaming my head off so loudly that by the time we landed I had no voice left for the interview.

'How could you tell I had my eyes closed?' I croaked.

'I have a little mirror in the front so I can see the face of the passenger. If they are going green or have fainted or are being sick I can see. I could see you had your eyes closed. And anyway you look like a screamer.' Charming.

****

My time with Tom was not to be this exhausting or adventurous. I did take him to watch the bungee jumpers. His little eyes focused on the bodies bouncing up and down and found it quite funny but I don't think he quite understood what it was all about. Me neither.

Together, we sought out the more gentle pursuits of taking a coach ride to the Abel Tasman Park to catch the boat at Kaiteriteri. The scenery was spectacular and the coach, not unsurprisingly, was full of families and OAPs. The younger crowd were probably doing what I had done on my previous visit. But our companions were all very lively and excellent company, passing Tom around like a bag of sweets.

We enjoyed our treks up to some of the waterfalls, seeing the wonderful countryside and learning about the history of the place. I took time to meet some of the local artists who are inspired by the region and have second homes here. All the artists and writers I met seemed to be inspired by the peace and tranquillity of the area.

On my first trip, my itinerary had included a trip to a vineyard in the nearby Central Otago region. The small vineyard seemed to be carved out from a rocky, steep-sided gorge which, according to the owner, 'maximised available warmth and was north facing to catch most of the sun'. The owner was a former broadcaster from the UK, where he had his own radio station and television show. He had been very successful in the UK but unhappy. To escape the rat race he had travelled to the other side of the earth. He knew a lot of people who had done the same, many of whom had set up their own vineyards too, producing some good wine.

This particular expatriate had moved to the South Island 10 years ago with his family, where he claimed that the 'living was easy and that life was sweet'. He was especially proud of his Pinot Noir, which had even won an award that year. But he admitted that he was starting to re-enter the rat race by default as wine production, like any business, is still a business, and when you run a business you have stress and deadlines. He felt he was starting to get into a rut again.

As we drank several bottles of his award-winning wine, we had long, deep, philosophical chats about the nature of happiness and the difference between being contented and being happy. I told him that I thought I could never be contented but I could be happy.

Though he had had wealth and a hectic lifestyle in England, it had not made him happy. Many people who came to New Zealand, he said, were seeking something. An escape. Or themselves. Or an escape from themselves. Some of his friends and family had found happiness in Queenstown, others had not. He said the secret is rarely to be found on the other side of the world, or in a greener field. It is in the person himself. He thought that you had to search into yourself, not travel the world. Some people do this and still don't find what they're looking for. I said I travelled because it broadened my horizons, not because I was escaping or wanted to find something.

Travel, especially through work, had taught me so much about myself. It put things into perspective and showed me that people who stand still in life, tend to stand still in their attitudes and don't grow spiritually, mentally or emotionally either. Travelling had shown me the impact of culture on people's attitudes to life, love and of course, children.

This struck me most when Tom was with me. It was the attitude of people we met that mattered, not the facilities. The cots, the blankets, the extra space on the plane, the heated baby food, were all nice but it was the common courtesy and the warmth of our welcome that really counted.

I returned to the vineyard for a second visit and introduced Tom to the owner. He smiled and sat my baby on his lap. Tom smiled his big wide smile and clapped and shook his head from side to side and showed off his two bottom teeth, of which he was very proud.

'Ah', he said, looking at Tom but talking to me, 'you've found the secret of happiness. You're one person who doesn't have to go to the other side of the world to find it.'

LESSON LEARNT IN NEW ZEALAND

Attitudes
The attitude of those you meet is far more important than the facilities they have to offer.

BALI

Seven Months

Six years ago, in 1994, I honeymooned in Bali. First we went to Singapore for a few days and then moved on to the island. The 'Island of the Gods' is made up of volcanic mountains, rice terraces, giant banyans, palm groves, lakes and rivers.

The wedding had been a stressful affair. I wasn't sure I was doing the right thing and neither was Tom's father. At that point Tom certainly wasn't a twinkle in anyone's eye. It was the one sunny day in September. Actually, it seemed to be the one sunny day of the year. My dress was tight and white. I hadn't eaten for days and looked thinner than Ally McBeal. I wore a hat and not a veil and ate nothing on the morning of the wedding. I downed a vodka and orange that morning and my cousin's husband gave me away as my dad – bless him – couldn't walk down the aisle with me.

The ceremony went well. There were lots of Tom's father's work colleagues there. There were lots of my parents' friends. Lots of his parents' friends. A few of our friends. The reception was held at the nearby Priory. It had wonderful grounds, the ancient building provided a lovely setting, and the weather held out.

The speeches were fine. We had allowed guests to bring children and babies. To those of you considering this, be picky. Determine which of your friends and relatives you can trust if they bring their children and which you can't. It's all to do with the parents and nothing to do with the child. Some parents know that as soon as their baby or child starts crying they should leave the church or reception straight away. And they do. Others will hold out until the child cries itself sick. Don't ask them if they would like to bring their children. Or better still, don't ask them. In our case, one of the guests hogged every photo opportunity by standing at the front with her baby girl. This meant many of our wedding photos looked like christening photos. Her christening photos.

We spent the night at a nearby inn with a four-poster and a stand-alone bath at the end of it. Next day we made our way through the

rain to the airport to be whisked to I didn't know where. I had left all the arrangements to Tom's father and a very good job he had made of them too. We spent three nights in Singapore, doing nothing but sleep. Then we had dinner at Raffles where I got really drunk and we talked about past boyfriends and girlfriends – not a wise thing to do on honeymoon, or at any other time for that matter. It was a relaxing honeymoon.

****

I returned to Bali with Tom with mixed feelings. My honeymoon there had not been the type of holiday that I was used to. I have never been someone who likes to stay in a hotel and exclusively use their facilities and restaurants. Why bother to go to a new place if you don't see much of it or meet the people whose country you are visiting?

You can go to expensive hotels anywhere in the world and they all offer wonderful facilities, service, extra special touches. But the place and the people make travel special, not the hotel. A good one is merely an added bonus at the end of a day's adventure.

The hotel in Bali where we stayed, the Oberoi in Kuta, is luxurious. It is not one building but a host of little villas sprinkled about a large exotic garden by a private beach. Each villa has its own verandah and outdoor bathroom. Exotic fruit, which I love, is delivered to the room each day; I didn't eat it all. I would store it away in the bottom of the wardrobe for future consumption, for a packed lunch or an excursion. A wonderful Balinese woman would replenish the bowl each day, only to discover it completely empty by the next morning. I think I must have been a hamster in a previous life.

The flight from Australia to Bali took just under eight hours from Sydney to Jakarta; it went without a hitch. The hours pass very quickly when the service is efficient and you find yourself with a sleepy baby who is quite happy. Tom slept and fed and studied his hands and feet several times. He had reached a feet-studying phase.

Since month four, his hands had fascinated him, his fingers in particular. He would wave them about in front of his nose, examining the detail of his palms. He would look in wonder at these things at the end of his arms, fascinated that he could make them move. But since we had been to Australia his interest had progressed to his feet. Like most babies, Tom was extremely flexible. He could, and often did, almost manage to put his feet behind his head. He would clap the soles of his feet together like hands in front of his face and study how his toes curled and uncurled. He giggled and laughed at their movement and at the discovery that he could control these new toys.

We arrived in Bali on time, tired, thirsty and ready for bed. Tom had slept a lot on the plane, but was still content in my arms, resting his heavy head on my shoulder and nuzzling his nose into my neck. Moments like that are simple but special.

The hotel had sent a limousine to meet us. We drove for about half an hour to reach the Oberoi. We were greeted there with wreaths of flowers: Tom even had a mini one made especially for him.

Tom's father met us at the hotel, having flown straight from London (20 hours 20 minutes).

We were offered a larger villa than our honeymoon one; this one had its own private walled terrace. As before, there were his and her CD players, a colour television and a good view of the beach and the sea beyond. Also we had a 'his and her' shower unit and the compulsory al fresco bath, big enough for five. The terrace on the private verandah had bougainvillaea hanging from the walls, and the heady scent of frangipani filled the air.

I sat Tom on the king-sized bed which was strewn with frangipani petals. The petals looked and smelt wonderful, and Tom had fun pulling them into even smaller pieces and we had fun picking them up after him.

The Oberoi could provide baby food for Tom if he wanted it, but at seven months I was still feeding him, the easiest and safest thing to do. I had brought canisters of powdered goat's milk just in case and powdered organic baby food. If he was to try anything new it would be the fruit, but nothing too exotic. I didn't want to give him a funny tummy unnecessarily.

We ordered a cab into the town of Kuta, which is a hippy hangout full of Australians. It is a great place in which to hang out and chill out and drink beer. There is a 'Hard Rock' Café and more street vendors selling sunglasses and lighters than tourists. The vendors bartered half-heartedly with the tourists who didn't get into the spirit of things but came alive again with those who did. I bought a pair of fake Armani sunglasses and I still have them to this day. They look better than the originals.

I couldn't find a cab for the return journey so we were advised to take a bus. There was a queue at the bus stop and the bus, when it eventually arrived, was already crowded. Then one of the weirdest things happened. We tried to get on but there wasn't a seat, so I stood with Tom. Well, they weren't having that. There was a fuss with the driver and a few of the passengers and about four people got up from their seats and offered two to Tom and me. They actually got off the bus, as it would have been too crowded with everyone standing. I didn't understand what was being said to me, but noticed that at each of the stops, if there was a woman with a baby, someone would automatically get up for her and offer the seat. In some cases, they would actually leave the bus, even though it wasn't their stop. I could see them waiting patiently by the stop for the next one as our bus left. It would be a long wait, as I later learnt that there were only about six a day. Imagine that happening in England.

Our time at the Oberoi was mostly spent relaxing by the pool, keeping in the shade and watching over Tom's every move. The tropical sun is obviously very hot and Tom didn't like direct sunlight anyway – he is not a sun-worshipper like his mum.

The hotel offers a massage service to guests and I had taken advantage of this on our honeymoon. I had overdosed on sun the day before and every glide, pinch and pummel of the masseur's hands was agony. This time I asked if he could massage Tom. I had been told in hospital that massage was very positive for a baby's health. The midwife had recommended it to relax the baby and encourage sleep, not that Tom had ever had any problem sleeping.

I was asked to take off Tom's nappy and put him down on his back. The heady combination of aromatherapy oils and heat made me feel quite dizzy. Rather than massaging Tom himself, the masseur then showed me how to do it myself. Very gently, I rubbed around his tummy and navel, up and down his fat little legs and thinner arms and then made little circles on his forehead. He smiled and then dozed. Then I was asked to turn Tom over and use the same strokes in a circular motion on his back and his bottom, which I think he quite liked. Then I very gently stroked him round the back of the neck area, which I knew he did like. Lastly, we did his feet and hands, blowing between the toes and the fingers and gently stroking up and down. Tom curled up in a foetal position, produced a golden fountain of pee and went to sleep.

****

Our next port of call was the Kupa Kupa Barong hotel in Ubud, up in the mountains. By that evening we were much cooler.

The village of Ubud is the centre of Bali's considerable artistic colony and contains the galleries of the most successful painters. We visited some of the exhibitions at Celuk, Danpasar and the Museum Puri Lukistan, where you can see paintings and sculptures on display in a hilltop garden. A surreal idea.

The Kupa Kupa Barong is another luxury resort but this time overlooks dramatic rice terraces rather than the idyllic beach setting of the Oberoi.

One other adventure of note in Bali was at the neighbouring hotel to the Kupa Kupa, the Amanpuri, one of the luxury hotels in the Aman group. It is spectacular: there is no other word for it. There are fabulous views over the rice terraces; a pool that looks as though it dissolves into the side of the hill; and rooms which are full of ornate statues. The graceful service is second to none.

We – my husband and I – had been there for lunch on our honeymoon. We couldn't afford to stay there, but lunch was fine. I wore my fake Armani glasses and something cream-coloured and skimpy and he wore his Ralph Lauren linen shirt and looked cool. We ate light, drank little and soaked up the atmosphere.

With Tom in tow, I thought they would turn us away. Not a bit of it. Our reception was charming and gracious. We chose a table in the shade and a cot was provided so that Tom could lie in it while we ate. Or if we wanted a high chair, they had one of those too. Hand carved by local craftsmen and with batique silk draped across the back and the sides, it resembled a mini-throne. Just imagine spilling porridge over that. I wanted to take one home with me.

Tom was in his element as he watched his two servants nibble at the rice crackers, while he sat, for once, higher than all he surveyed. He sighed. He actually sighed a big, self-satisfied sigh. Bali, I felt, was better second time round for me.

LESSONS LEARNT IN BALI

1. Babies add another dimension to travel
Unless I had taken Tom to Bali, I would not have been aware of the reverence for mothers and young children. Tom's presence enhanced my experience of the island in more ways than one.

2. Babies and heat
Be careful with babies and extreme temperatures. Dehydration is a serious problem and it is obviously very important to keep children in the shade all the time, especially when they are very young. This means no trekking out into the midday sun. It's best to visit places like Bali, or anywhere else in the Far East, during the cooler seasons – during our winter – when it is not too humid or too hot.

3. Seats being offered
Don't expect to be offered a seat wherever you travel. It is an added bonus if you are. If you think along these lines, you will try to travel as light as you can with arms free (buy a decent front carrier); don't weigh yourself down with bags full of toys, and things to stimulate or comfort the baby.

ISLE OF MAN

Seven Months

Not the sexiest place to go, I thought. It was August, so the weather should be good, but it had just turned very autumnal. My brief was to interview Norman Wisdom at his home on the Isle of Man. He rarely visits London, so I would have to go to him. (For those of you who don't know who Norman Wisdom is, I have no time for you.)

Norman Wisdom was the comfort food of my childhood. He took the lead in films such as The Square Peg, The Early Bird and Trouble in Store. He is multi-talented – a singer, a dancer, a comedian, an actor. A performer and a real pro. When I met him at his home (which he designed himself) I discovered that he is also a genuine, rather lovely man.

When I was a little girl he made me laugh so much that tears would stream down my face and my sides ache. He made me feel even more positive about a world that I already thought was wonderful and good. Not many films do that for me these days.

Norman would always play the underdog. He might be bullied and vilified but he always won through in the end with his determination, quick wit and sense of humour and fair play. He always got the girl, although she was usually twice his height. And he was always kind to animals in his films, which was a real selling point for me.

I was in the Isle of Man on behalf of Jazz FM Travel Guide. I had been working on the project for months. I had thought of it when I was five months pregnant just after the trip to the Yukon with Discovery Channel. I wanted a new challenge. So I approached someone on the board of directors of Jazz FM and made my pitch.

I found a sponsor, an excellent producer, Chris, and a team of correspondents who were enthusiastic, professional and very good at what they did. By this time Tom was seven months old, he was starting to get heavy and be very curious about the sights and sounds around him. He couldn't be left to sit on a bed, even if you placed him in the middle of it. He would somehow make his way to the edge and fall off. I couldn't get a babysitter for the days I was due to be in the Isle of

Man, so I decided to take Tom with me although it was a working trip. For once, my attentions would have to be elsewhere, and, unlike our other destinations, we would be in a place I hadn't visited before.

I had never taken Tom on a working trip overseas. To numerous meetings in London, yes, but never overseas. Until then, our trips together had been purely for pleasure, enabling us to explore places at my own pace and in my own time. Most of them I had already been to for Classic FM, so I knew my way around. But the Isle of Man was completely new to me, as I said, and I had to deliver a pre-recorded radio broadcast on the place and the people in 24 hours with a baby in tow. When I told the Isle of Man PR about my intention to take Tom he was very helpful and said it wouldn't be a problem.

I took the train into town with Tom's dad, who always catches the 6.15 every morning from Chelmsford to Liverpool Street Station. At that time, the train was not crowded and Tom was happy to stare at people and not whinge and gurgle which he was starting to do more often. Commuters were too tired at that early hour to scowl.

Next we took a cab to Paddington to catch the Heathrow Express. The cab driver asked me how old Tom was, if he was a boy or a girl and then told me about his grandchildren, their eating and sleeping habits, how he disapproved of the way his daughter brought them up etc, etc. I told him to listen to the Jazz FM Travel Guide at 7pm on Mondays starting soon.

Travelling for Classic FM, especially if it was for only an overnight stay, I would usually take just one small piece of hand luggage. A clean pair of knickers, plus my microphone and DAT recorder and that would be it, apart from some reading material maybe. I would be on and off planes quickly without fuss, missed connections or lost luggage. Having a baby changed all that.

For a start, I had taken Tom in his car seat. The PR would chauffeur us around the island for the duration, and Tom needed to be in a car seat. It was heavy and unwieldy, and Tom, at nearly 22 pounds, was no lightweight either. I had brought his milk, bottles, a toy, and a change of clothes. I had nothing for myself apart from my tape recorder and microphone which I had nearly forgotten in my anxiety to make sure I had everything for my son. So getting out of the cab and on to the platform was not easy. Tom was heavy, the bags were heavy and no one helped. To be fair, I didn't ask anyone to help. I just sulked, expecting my thunderous looks to shame those around me. It didn't work. This never happened overseas, I thought.

The Heathrow Express is clean, quick and efficient. There are baby-changing facilities on the train, which runs punctually. A television screen tells you when you are about to depart, and when you will arrive at the airport. I have nothing but praise for the service.

Domestic departures take off from Terminal One at Heathrow, which I hate. There is a limited variety of shops and the queues to check in are long. I had to collect my ticket at the airport as the notice was too short to send it by post. Otherwise I could have checked in at Paddington and avoided that queue. When I eventually arrived at the front of the queue, I was told that the car seat either had to go in oversized baggage or I would have to take Tom in it through to the departure gate where the cabin crew would take it from me. But it was so heavy I wanted to get rid of it as soon as possible. The seat that is, not Tom. The oversized luggage area was over at the other end of the concourse and the queue there was even longer. So I struggled back to the check-in desk and the departures lounge once more. Now I had to co-ordinate my efforts through the bit where it beeps if you have anything metallic on you. I put the bag and car seat through the conveyor belt and emptied my pockets of change. I handed my mobile phone over to the guy pushing the luggage through for inspection. The monitor bleeped. A woman searched me for bombs, knives and drugs but didn't find anything. She did smile at Tom. I collected my bag and the car seat and made my way up a long corridor to the departure area. No trolleys were allowed so the aerobics class came in useful.

I don't believe it. I've forgotten my mobile. I went up to someone who looked like an air hostess. (Their outfits look so casual and trendy these days, it is difficult to tell whether they are or not.) I explained I had left my mobile at the inspection area and she told me there wasn't enough time for me to go back for it: they would send it on the next day. I was only there for a day, I explained. She tutted. Obviously English. She said she would go back to get it. What type was it? A Nokia. She returned five minutes later. There are two Nokias – could you please ring your number so we can identify which one it is. I did, and she rushed back a few minutes later with a smile, frantically waving a phone at me.

'I'm surprised there was more than one phone left behind', I said.

'It happens all the time. We had 53 yesterday.'

A recommendation. Just like the last part of The Generation Game, when you see things going past you on a conveyor belt, make sure you remember what you have seen and remember to say what is missing at the other end.

To say the flight on Manx Airlines was cramped would be an understatement. Sardines would have had more room in their tin. Tom didn't seem to mind, although he cried a bit at the beginning of the journey which made the businessman sitting next to me smile. Obviously he wasn't English.

The Isle of Man is a base for many corporate banking and insurance companies. The plane was therefore full of male suits and only a few women and children. They all seemed quite content. No scowls. Thankfully Tom, despite the squash, was so tired that he soon dozed off. So did I.

The weather was foul when we arrived, after a trip which had taken about an hour and a half. The steps from the plane were slippery and narrow and Tom looked as worried as I did. I had dressed for a sunny day with a long flowing dress, as the weather that day in the Isle of Man had been forecast as fair. It wasn't and I looked a complete twit.

The airport terminal was small, but the luggage collection area was not too far to walk and I picked up the seat and the bag (making sure I had the mobile on me this time) without fuss.

Daphne the PR looked welcoming but anxious when I came through the doors holding Tom. 'Ah, you've brought him. I didn't know if you were going to bring him.' She looked flustered.

'Sorry, but I thought it would be interesting to see if I could take Tom on a job with me.'

I didn't ask her to carry anything. It wasn't her problem that I had brought this baby with me, I thought. We made our way to her car, a blue Renault Scenic. Lovely, but rather excessive for me, Tom, and a bag.

Norman was expecting us at 11.30. The flight had been delayed and so we had to make our way straight there before checking in at the hotel. Daphne had forgotten the map, but had been to Norman's house before. Once. A year ago.

We got lost. The mobile worked on some hills and not on others. We found one on which it did work and got directions.

Norman Wisdom lives in a large, spectacular house, with extensive views over fields and meadows. The rooms are large and the furniture is laden with trophies and mementoes and pictures of him with other famous people. He is charming, and has a wonderful voice for radio, with deep, soft tones. I asked him about his travels and favourite destinations in the world. He told me how much he liked the Isle of Man and all about India where he had served in the army. He described how he had got into acting and how Marilyn Monroe had kissed him on the lips. 'Properly, not a peck.' He told me how Noël Coward had also taken a shine to him. But there had been no kissing.

When we met he was trying to get a film, Adam and Evil, off the ground. 'And it will only cost £4 million, which is not a lot of money for a film,' he told me repeatedly and reassuringly.

We left Tom in the Renault asleep. Daphne went out every five minutes to check if he was still OK. He was. But she brought him in anyway for a photo to be taken of him with Norman and me. Tom was brilliant. He didn't throw up over my hero, but just smiled and cooed at Norman just as I had done when I had been interviewing him a few minutes earlier.

No other interviews were planned for that day, but I needed to talk to some people to get a sense of the place – the history, the culture, the cats. Ah, yes, Manx cats from the Isle of Man. Did you know that Manx cats have no tails not because (as the rumour goes) they were too slow for Noah's Ark, and literally nearly missed the boat and had their tails cut off by the doors closing. They have no tails because they suffer from a form of bone disease, which causes them to have no tails and very runny tummies. Not as romantic, eh? We visited a refuge where hundreds of cats were kept and heard the horror stories of how they had been ill-treated before they were rescued. How nasty boys attach fireworks to their legs and watch them scream with pain. How some people refuse to the have the males neutered and then bash the kittens on the head instead of preventing their birth in the first place.

There were cats everywhere in the refuge. They had even invaded the kitchen. They were on top of the cupboards, under the chairs and tables, on and around the sink, hanging from the window sill, even in one case sticking out of a flowerpot, bottom up. All shapes and sizes and colours.

And would one miaow for me and my microphone? Just a little squeak? Or even a loud purr would do? No. Not once in the kitchen of 100 cats did any of them make a sound. So often when an animal, especially one that would usually make a lot of noise (cats, dogs, geese, ducks), sees a microphone, they freeze. The cats froze.

The Isle of Man, as well as being famous for its cats, is increasingly used as a location for films. Waking Ned had been filmed there the previous year, and Relative Values with Julie Andrews, Colin Firth and Stephen Fry was being filmed while I was visiting. The actors were all based in a mansion once owned by racehorse owner Robert Sangster, and built on the site of an old nunnery. It took two months to complete the film in and around the building.

The art director (a credit on the screen I would previously have ignored completely) had to work wonders. He had to transform a building which had been decorated in a very seventies style into something out of the fifties. Whoever he was, he succeeded brilliantly. Much of the original woodwork in the house had been painted over in white gloss, and the art director had had it restored to its original splendour. The walls had been covered with wonderful fabrics, and the furnishings chosen were exquisite.

One of the actors I interviewed on set told me most people think the money in films goes to the actors, but a lot of it goes into providing the right background and setting. In the forthcoming weeks the art director would have to turn the Isle of Man into Hollywood and the South of France. Rather him than me, I thought.

I wanted to interview all the cast for my programme, but had not given sufficient notice to do so. In the end, the lead actor, Andrew Edgerton, did allow me to interview him. He was very handsome, sweet and interviewed well. I hope he becomes extremely famous one day. Meanwhile Tom was in the Renault with Daphne, who was almost getting used to entertaining a baby.

By this stage I had interviewed eight people in the past eight hours and by 9 pm had eaten nothing more than two pears. Tom had eaten better than his mother, with dishes of baby rice and garden vegetables (organic and GM free) and goat's milk to wash it down. Yum.

I was tired and hungry and looking forward to an evening with Daphne at the Waterford Restaurant which was owned by Kevin Woodford, the television personality who is a chef. Or is he the chef who is a television personality?

But the hotel let me down. There was no nanny available although I had asked that morning. I didn't make a fuss. They had been kind at the hotel, despite failing to provide a cot. The lift was bloody awful: small and dirty and not enough room to swing a Manx cat even if he had a tail to swing by. So I had to take Tom to this romantic, candlelit restaurant where couples were canoodling in corners and everything was peace and quiet except for some classical music playing gently in the background.

Tom sat in his car seat, staring at the candles. He was transfixed.

The restaurant is lovely. The menu is superb. Fish: I love fish. I ordered smoked salmon and queenies (baby scallops), followed by poached salmon. Just as in Finland, if the dessert had had salmon in it, I would have ordered that. I ordered a glass of wine too, a treat as I don't drink much alcohol these days.

Tom started to whinge. A long, wind-up squeal that got progressively louder and more irritating and more screech-like. Like an owl with toothache. I picked him up. Talked to him. Cuddled him and put him down again. He screeched. I wanted my food. I was hungry and tired and wanted to chat to Daphne about her impending wedding to her love of ten years. Tom continued to make his presence felt. I was sorry for the other couples, as it wasn't very romantic with a baby screeching. Eventually I took him out and put him in the Renault and sang a few songs, very badly, which always works with him. He fell asleep. We would only be about another five minutes. I wouldn't have dessert but just finish my main course.

Five minutes later Daphne noticed a police van parking outside the restaurant. On an island the size of Man (13 miles wide by 33 miles long), this does not usually happen at 9.30 at night on a working day. We went downstairs. There were about ten people surrounding the Renault, including a bemused-looking policeman. Tom was fine – a bit nervous about all the faces peering at him, but OK apart from that.

'Whose baby is this?'

'Mine.'

'Can I have your name and address? How long have you been away from the vehicle?'

'Five minutes.'

'No, you haven't', one of the onlookers butted in. I didn't look at her. Daphne did. 'The baby's been in there for over ten minutes. We've been waiting here for ten minutes.'

'Well, it's not my place to tell people how to bring up a child', the policeman said, and left it at that. He went off with my name and address and Daphne's details but said no more. The onlookers disappeared and so did the idea of having a quiet dinner and some girly chat.

This trip had probably been my worst ever. This was not because the Isle of Man is a bad place to take children. On the contrary, it is extremely good with them, and everyone seems very friendly, hospitable and helpful. Indeed, the island sells itself as a place to take the family and there are plenty of things to do and see. There is a serenity about the place which is very special.

No, it was bad for me because Tom was reaching the age when it was starting to get more difficult to travel with him. Ironically, when he was starting to appreciate the things around him, and wanting to explore for himself, I was able to enjoy myself less and concentrate less on my work.

On this trip I had been with people who, rather than seeing me as a holiday-maker, or just a traveller, were seeing me as a journalist on location, working. Although I had tried to anticipate this by warning the PR that I was bringing a baby, the whole point about babies is that they are unpredictable. It is increasingly difficult, as they grow older, to combine catering for their needs and demands with those of a working journalist, as I found to my cost.

LESSONS LEARNT IN THE ISLE OF MAN

1. With age comes weight

The older the baby gets, the heavier he becomes and the more difficult to carry. Sounds obvious, doesn't it? But don't underestimate the extra weight of a baby between three, five and seven months. They grow quickly and are more demanding each day. Keep your travels short and sweet and complete them soon – preferably before the baby reaches double figures (in months that is).

2. Business and pleasure

The Isle of Man trip demonstrated how difficult it can be to mix business and take a baby unless you have a nanny. It's not really fair on the baby or you.

3. The generation game

New mothers are supposed to lose their memories a bit when they give birth. The best thing to do when going through security at airports is to keep the amount of hand luggage small and your pockets empty, preferably with everything in one bag. That way your mobile phone might not go astray.

SENEGAL

Nine Months

I didn't plan to take Thomas to Africa before the age of one. I wanted the Isle of Man to be the last trip. Because of the risk of infection, the doctor had advised me against travelling to South America and India, and told me to be careful about Africa.

At nine months, Tom was still not crawling, but sitting up he had mastered beautifully. He clapped when you said clap. And clapped when you didn't. He waved with both hands and looked sideways at you just like Princess Diana used to do. Fortunately he had inherited his father's easygoing nature and was quite content to let everyone else do any fussing for him.

He had also identified those who could be pushovers amongst his relations. I was definitely not one of them. I was horrible. Definitely. It was just as well that he could now hold his own bottle, operate his own spoon, and sit up alone. He also had a nice line in conversation – ba ba ba and ga ga ga – and I think he even called my name once.

****

Out of all the countries I had travelled to as a working journalist, before Tom was born, Senegal had been the most enchanting and poignant trip. There had been about eight of us. One was another radio journalist, from BBC Scotland, who always seemed to be after exactly the same interview as me. Or was I after exactly the same interview as him? Anyway – we were competitive. Then there was a journalist from *Hello!* magazine, Susan, who was great fun and brilliant company, as she still is.

I hadn't told my other half where I was going – or even that I was going anywhere at all. I knew he wouldn't want me to go. He thought all my trips were jollies, all play and no work, and that I occasionally switched on my tape recorder if I felt like it.

The trip was brilliantly organised. It was probably one of the best press trips I have ever been on in terms of the strength and variety of material I returned with and the friendships I made.

On the first night in Dakar I rang my husband.

'Where are you?'

'Er, I've had to go on an assignment.'

'Where?'

'Just to Paris.'

'You don't sound as though you are in Paris. Where are you?'

Damn the time difference – there was a time delay in the speech.

'Well, I'm in Senegal. You know in Afri ...'

'Yes, I know where Senegal is, you silly cow.' (Or words to that effect.) 'What the **** are you doing in Senegal?'

'I'm working.'

'Yeah, right.'

'Yes, and I'm with lots of other people so I'm perfectly safe.'

'Yeah, right.'

'And I'll be back in ten days time.'

'Yeah, right.'

'Love you.'

'Mmm. Don't do anything silly.'

Click.

One reason I hadn't said where I was going was that refugees from Sierra Leone had been trying to dock in Dakar that winter, and there were rumours that they were carrying typhoid. Headstrong as ever, I had decided I would still go.

I had read up on Senegal before I left. I learnt that the Senegalese are very tall, very beautiful people. The west coast of Africa is where you find the interesting tribes, the east coast the interesting animals. As Senegal is a French colony, French is widely spoken there. Direct flights go from Paris, but none from London. We flew with Air France, which was great.

Unlike other trips where everything merged into everything else, distinct pictures and sounds associated with Senegal still linger in my mind. Three stand out in particular.

There is an island called the Ile de Gore just a short boat ride from Senegal's capital, Dakar. The small port is busy and fascinating. The boat ride was quick and we were met by an English-speaking guide who led us to our first stopping place.

The Ile de Gore, for those who don't know, is the place where the African slaves were held before they were shipped in their tens of thousands to the Americas. They were kept cramped in appalling conditions. The women were raped and so were the men. They were badly beaten and those who survived the beatings invariably failed to survive the crossing, where the space was even more confined than their quarters had been on the island. The female slaves were frequently made pregnant by the white (and African, it must be said) masters, and these children were also sold into slavery – or drowned in the dead of night, thrown down a well or into the sea. At least they were saved from the misery of slavery.

The island echoed the sadness of its past. What made it even more poignant is that it was absolutely beautiful. There was a stillness about it. Bougainvillaea grew against every whitewashed building. The wealthy French who holiday in Senegal have built holiday cottages on the island. It was peaceful and tranquil and there were interesting and good restaurants dotted about the place. But reminders of the slavery were present on almost every street. By covering it with flowers, Mother Nature and time had attempted to hide the past, tarnishing the edges of some chain or manacle so that it looked like one of those ornaments you might buy in a trendy art shop in Chelsea for £100 or more.

We were led to the place where the slaves were kept. The guide there could not speak English, which is always a problem for a radio journalist as translated voice-over doesn't work properly. It can be done, though, and our guide said he would translate for me. I turned my tape recorder on.

The one thing I really love about being a radio journalist is that it demands that you listen to every word that is being said to you. Not only must you listen to make sure the material is interesting but that the sound quality is clear, that there are no pops or any hissing. So you listen intently to every word, which is what I did on the Ile de Gore.

The guide described the conditions in which the slaves were kept. How the numbers that were taken from these shores will never really be known, but that they were so vast that it is the predominant reason for Africa's poverty today. The guide was passionate. His expressive French voice resonated in the warm, quiet air. About thirty tourists stood with us, listening to his words and those of the translators.

Our translator echoed the guide's passion.

'*Tout le monde* … ' 'Everybody always talks about the Jews, and how they were ill-treated … '*Mais, les Africains* … 'But the plight of the Africans went on for decades and we will never know the numbers that were taken away. Millions.'

'*Ne personne* …' 'Nobody ever talks about the Africans and they suffered longer and far more than the Jews …'

'*Alors, je vais* …' 'Well, I'm going to shout about the Africans, and how they were ill-treated, and savaged until the day I die. Do you hear that, until the day I die …'

It's funny, but listening to the words through the headphones – so strong and so passionate – it felt as though I was his own private audience. I have never forgotten that man's face, or the island.

****

Another memorable episode occurred a few days later.

The group were shattered. We had been in a dusty bus for hours on end each day, but the trip had been very productive. I had recorded some wonderful voices at the local market and interesting interviews, but I knew there was more. This place was so rich. So real. There was nothing artificial about any of it.

Our tired and irritable group arrived at this paradise by the sea. We each had our own little hut and were given the option of having what the press trip itinerary prosaically calls 'free time'. In free time, you can do other interviews or you can relax. The group, for the most part, wanted to relax. I, of course, asked if there was anything interesting to record.

'There is a monastery near here where the monks sing Gregorian chants.' As soon as I heard this I knew I wanted to go. Apparently it was about an hour's drive away, and mass was at 8am. This meant we would have to leave at 6am, and it would cost about £30 for a driver to take us there.

'Will anyone go with me?' (Please God, don't let the BBC Scotland man come, I thought.)

'I'll come', BBC Scotland man piped up.

At least we could share the cost.

'I'll come.' Lindsay from *The Lady* magazine was the third.

Only three takers. The others looked at us as though we were completely mad. We were completely mad.

I didn't sleep well. Mosquitoes buzzed in and out of my netting, dive-bombing my nose, and occasionally hitting it. I woke up looking like a teenager with hyperactive hormones.

The trip was long and dusty and everyone was too cross to speak. No one said anything to me, just looked at me as if to say 'This is your fault. You made us do this'. That included the driver.

After about forty minutes we arrived at this tiny chapel in the middle of nowhere. The guide had overestimated the time not because of the lack of traffic, but because, invariably, the driver has difficulty finding the road as the dust storms cover it up.

The chapel was already crowded with locals. All the women wore hats or scarves around their heads. Everyone looked smart. Sunday best. We, on the other hand, looked like something the cats on the Ile de Gore had dragged in. We smelt bad too.

After about ten minutes the choir came in, about 10 of them, followed by about another ten carrying instruments – drums, sitars, others I can't remember the name of.

Then the singing started. The chants. Deep and low at the beginning, like a storm brewing up, and then bursting into the full crescendo of the chorus. The congregation didn't join in. They seemed as mesmerised as we were, happy just to stare. The monks in their cream robes sang as the musicians beat on their African drums. The sound was totally hypnotic in the heat of the African wilderness. No one said a word. I recorded the whole sixty-minute service, stopping only when my tape ran out and made a very rude beeping sound during the one time the singers had stopped for breath.

Years later, I still play these voices sometimes at home when I'm tired, or unhappy, or restless. I remember the place so clearly. Lindsay and BBC Scotland man thanked me for making them get up at 6am to take that journey. I told them to tell the others it had been nothing special. If they had known they would have kicked themselves for missing something so magical and unique.

The last special Senegal memory concerns Domaine de Naning. Domaine de Naning is like a Noah's Ark on dry land. A man who looks like God and talks like God has developed a sanctuary for animals in the middle of the desert – of which Senegal has a great deal. He breeds all sorts of animals, including alligators and crocodiles. As guests on his Ark you are allowed to visit his animals, but so vast is the area, you do so on a bicycle. We met the chimpanzees, who ate the hat of one of the other journalists and nearly pulled her hair out as well, and all sorts of other animals. All of them looked the part, but as usual would resolutely shut up as soon as I put a microphone to their beak or mouth.

I was getting rather frustrated by this vow of silence, at the end of a very unproductive day, when we came upon the crocodiles. Would they snap their jaws for me? I would have to get quite close to find out.

It's not as if they don't bite. I know they do.

'There are baby crocodiles we breed over here', said our guide, trying to be helpful.

We were led to a little paddock and shown into this area where there were about five baby crocodiles no bigger than five inches long – about as long as my hand from wrist to finger-tip. They were wonderful. Everyone took pictures. But they didn't make a sound. Great.

'Do they make any sound?' I said, expecting the answer.

'Yes, they do, they make a little squeak when you pinch them just behind the jaw.'

'Could you, please, very gently, pinch them behind the jaw then, and I'll record the squeak?'

He did, and this tiny crocodile, that would one day become one of the beautiful monsters we had just seen snapping into a dead sheep five minutes before, let out a little yap. And another. And another. And do you know what? It cried. Big tears came from its eyes. The genuine thing: crocodile tears.

It was moments like these that I wanted to share with Tom.

****

Tom was a pro at the airport and aeroplane scene by now. He was in his element. Dakar airport was just as I remembered it, very busy, but we were met by a guide. I wanted to see all the things I had seen on my previous trip.

The Ile de Gore hadn't changed. Tom was fascinated by the cats, which prowled everywhere. I listened to the guide, this time paying more attention to what became of the children and the babies and clutching Tom closer and closer until, like the baby crocodile, he began to yap.

We visited the special monastery in the middle of nowhere, where they still sang the chants. I was so very pleased they did. So many things are discontinued or destroyed by over-commercialisation and something like this is so difficult to recapture once it is lost. Tom sat on my lap, silent as I had been many years before, and listened intently to the drums. He even swayed and bounced up and down to the beat. Good sense of rhythm, my son.

'You're the one with the noisy tape recorder,' said the monk, who remembered me from all those years ago.

'Yes, that's me.'

Finally we went to Domaine de Naning, which is actually ideal for families. I would recommend it without reservation to anyone wanting to take their child on a voyage of exploration, albeit not too close to the crocodiles. The man who owned it had a slightly longer white beard and slightly more animals on his Ark. The 'baby' crocodile who had yapped for me was now slightly bigger and I wasn't going to ask anyone to pinch him behind his jaws. I did, however, show Tom another baby crocodile. Aware that he might seem a tasty morsel to this whipper of a snapper, I kept him at a safe distance.

LESSONS LEARNT IN SENEGAL

1. Insurance
Make sure you take out good insurance. For example standard holiday insurance may exclude pregnancy-related problems. If you are seeking insurance to cover a holiday while pregnant or with a very young baby, ask a broker or contact the Association of British Insurers (020 7600 3333).

2. Injections and alternative medicine
Prepare in advance if you are to give your child alternative means of combating infection and disease. Homeopathy, for example, can take time to work – perhaps months to get into the system.

3. The internet
Surf the net. There are sites which are useful: www.babydirectory.com is one of many out there. www.family-travel.co.uk is, in my opinion, the best.

4. First year travel
Travel a lot in the first year if you have the time, the energy and the inspiration. It's the easiest time to do it and also gets your baby used to planes, trains, taxis, airports and stations.

AND FINALLY

Have Baby Will Travel is not a reference book. It is an account of journeys I made as an independent traveller and radio journalist before I had Tom, and then those with Tom when I retraced my steps to see if and how the experience changed for better or worse.

The experiences were not better or worse. They were different.

I am not usually on holiday in any of the countries I visit. On most occasions I was there on business to interview people, with a tight itinerary of meeting this person, seeing this sight, getting involved in that activity. It is not impossible to continue to do these things with a baby in tow (see the Isle of Man chapter) but it is not easy. You really need someone on call all the time.

I learnt from my own travels and from speaking to others about their experiences, that you can take a very young baby almost anywhere in the world, but in order to make the journey as stress-free as possible you must adapt and prepare. Common sense, really.

I have been surprised by the different attitudes of people I have met in the various countries. By turns we were shown overwhelming enthusiasm (Italy), apathy (England) or basic common sense (Sweden).

What makes travelling enjoyable and even enhances the experience when you are with a baby is that in some countries at least, the baby creates an opportunity to meet people who would not normally start up a conversation. The baby is a talking point and people will stop to talk to you. Perversely, and perhaps rather sadly, in our own country, people will try to ignore you. This has only been in my relatively limited experience, but judge for yourself. Go on the London Underground and see if anyone helps you with your push chair. Nine times out of ten it will be a tourist who will offer to help.

Contrast this with the Paris or Hong Kong metro, where they will be fighting to help you. Perhaps it's a cultural issue. Or perhaps it's just an example of good and bad manners.

Travelling with a baby heightens your senses and awareness of your surroundings. When I travelled with Tom on second visits to places, in most cases the experience was completely different because my perspectives and values had changed. I was aware of different things. The safety of trains and cleanliness of airports. Common courtesy and manners. How people on the street reacted. If they smiled. How many other women had babies with them, and how they were treated. How quickly people offered to help. And how often people ignored you.

Obviously becoming a mother had changed me, as much as it had changed people's perception of me as a traveller. Perhaps I was treated differently because I expected to be treated differently.

Travelling with Tom certainly made me appreciate places and people in a different way. I noticed their patience, their hospitality, their care for the elderly and the young. These qualities became important to me. As an independent traveller, I had been impatient for the elderly woman to cross the road. Did I ever help anyone up the escalator with a push chair, or down a flight of stairs on the Underground? Never. Not once. Yet now, when I see someone in that predicament, I jump to their aid.

Perhaps London is a fast city not designed for mothers with babies. But so, in many ways, are Hong Kong and Toronto, and not once did I feel abandoned or left to my own devices when I needed help in either of these cities.

What has been most striking is how relatively difficult it is to travel with a baby in my own country. On the trains, on the Underground, by car, at road side cafés, in restaurants.

In certain places, to be fair, services are improving. Even the railways are becoming more mother-and-baby focused, realising that there is a potential market here.

Health clubs and supermarkets in this country have already identified this growing market. Clubs like Holmes Place, Cannons and Fitness First, which have clubs throughout the UK, offer very good crèche facilities for mums who want to get back into shape, or just stay in shape.

Sainsbury's and Tesco have excellent changing facilities in most of their large supermarkets, and their own 'baby club' magazines. If only other retail outlets would follow their lead.

Is the English weather to blame for our generally grumpy attitude to babies? I don't think so. Yes, the warmer climates of Spain, Italy and the Latin American countries do also correspond to what I call the 'baby friendly factor'. The people are as passionate about babies as they are about life and food and living in general. But Canada is a very cold country for most of the year. Sweden and Finland are not known for their boiling hot summers, while winters are positively sub-zero. All are much 'baby-friendlier' countries than England.

Perhaps it is our education. Perhaps we are taught subliminally that women with babies should neither be seen nor heard, at least until the baby has turned into a toddler, and even then only when they have the good manners to know when to shut up.

****

I found that the best time to travel with a baby is in its first year. Don't wait until your child can crawl or walk or say no. It will become increasingly difficult to travel as he grows older.

There are no hard and fast rules about which airlines to travel with, which airports to fly from, which hotels to stay in and which countries to avoid. The only hard and fast rule is to do your research.

As I learnt from experience, master the art of being a charming bully to ensure that you get what you want, when you want it and where you want it. Follow the Girl Guide motto: Be Prepared. Book that seat with more space on the long haul flight. Let the restaurant know exactly how old your baby is and if high chairs are no good.

The maxim 'happy mother, happy baby' is such a true one. Stressed mother, stressed baby. If you are cool and happy, so will your baby be.

In that first year, your baby may not appreciate the journeys in the same way that you do, but he will be far more stimulated by travelling than by staying at home, watching daytime television and playing with toys. And so, I am sure, will you. If Tom could speak, then I think he would tell me that he has appreciated what we have done together. Perhaps when he is older, he may want to retrace the same steps again – with his children.

CELEBRITY TIPS AND ANECDOTES

During the course of my work and while I have been writing this book, I have had the opportunity to ask a number of people for their own thoughts and experiences of travelling with their own or other people's young children. Here is what some of them had to say.

JON SNOW: Newsreader and Channel 4 News anchor
Favourite places: Grenada and Australia

I think you have to realise that a baby is simply an extension of mum and a little bit of dad. If you are sure about what you want to do and where you want to go – just do it, the child will fit in. The moment you begin to organise everything from the child's perspective you have lost the point. A child, especially a baby, has no view of anything. All it wants is you and to be sure of you. If you are confident about what you are doing, the child will be happy. I am now the father of teenage children and I would say, from experience, that the best and easiest time to travel with children is during their first year of life.

The first time I ever travelled with our first baby, we took her to Paris when she was just one month old. It was a bit of a disaster as we were not at all confident with her. Our baby became very distressed, but the air hostess was amazing. She took it all in her stride and our daughter soon calmed down. After that everything was plain sailing – absolutely brilliant!

ALAN WHICKER: Author, television presenter and interviewer
Favourite place: Easter Island

My tip is to make sure you are at the other end of the plane when people are travelling with their babies. I've just returned from a trip where there was a man looking after two babies and I was full of admiration for him. It's just that I wanted to admire him from afar.

CLAIRE RAYNER: Agony aunt, author
Favourite place: The Mediterranean

With babies, always remember smell and light: the senses. The most important thing to remember about babies is to appeal to their senses. When travelling, get a handkerchief and rub it on yourself, on your arm or on your chest, and then allow the baby to hold it. If they have to be held by someone else in the airport or at the station, or whenever there are hold-ups, they will smell you on the handkerchief and be comforted. Also, if you are staying in a hotel, try to make sure that the window and door are in exactly the same position in the hotel room as they are at home: this way the baby won't feel so disorientated. As for me travelling when my children were babies – we didn't. We were too poor. But my children have since travelled all over the place with their own and I think they have benefited from the experience. Very relaxed parents when travelling produce very relaxed children, in my experience.

WILLIAM DALRYMPLE: Travel writer
Favourite place: India

We travelled with our children to India when they were only three weeks old. They are so portable when they are that young and on the breast. The worst time to travel with a baby is probably when it is about 13 months when it is putting everything into its mouth. You must be careful and vigilant at that age particularly. The best thing to entertain babies when they aren't sleeping or feeding is movement. Our children loved trains in particular and we travelled a lot by train in India. This always made them fall asleep. As children get older, outdoor attractions such as forts, castles, beaches or anything to do with animals (our very young children found monkeys or elephants particularly fascinating to watch) are a good source of entertainment. Forget art galleries and museums: you can't risk the crying in places where silence or near silence is part of the package, and it ruins it for other people. Go alone on that one.

COLONEL JOHN BLASHFORD SNELL: Chairman of the Scientific Exploration Society
Favourite places: Mongolia and New Zealand

I have an adopted grandchild who is Nepalese and a grandson, Fat Jack, whom I plan to take on expeditions. You must always be so careful with babies and young children near water. You hear of so many tragedies when small children drown, even in England in swimming pools. Whether in a developed or an undeveloped country it is so important to teach your children to swim. They are never too young to learn. In my experience, the further you get from civilisation, the nicer people are to you and your children.

When my daughters were very young, I took them to Nepal. I had been asked to survey a river to see if it was passable by white water rafting. No one did white water rafting in Nepal in those days so it was quite difficult to find people to do it with me. Eventually, we found some people to come with us, and a couple of sherpas, so my family and several others went down the river. It was all going well, until I made a stupid mistake. I got my oar stuck between two rocks, pulled hard and it snapped and hit my nose. My elder daughter tried to comfort me, while the little one tried to find something to cheer me up. When I opened my eyes, I saw through the mist of blood that my daughter was presenting me with a human skull, with bits of flesh still hanging from it.

'Look what I brought you daddy,' she said. You see they cremate people in the river and this was the remains of one of the cremations. I put the skull back in the river and told my daughter to wash her hands. The journey got quite dangerous in the end and even the sherpas eventually gave up. They told me that they would climb Everest any time but that they thought this journey was madness.

My father and mother did a tremendous amount of travelling so I think it is in my blood. Father was an Anglican parson, ordained in Dunedin, and mother was an outdoorsy sort of person. They had lots of adventures. They set up a church in the South Island of New Zealand, and travelled a lot from there. I went into the army, and travelled a lot as a Royal Engineer, getting paid to do it. It was a bit like travel journalism really, but we had to blow people up as well.

DESMOND MORRIS: Author of *The Naked Ape*, *The Human Animal*, *Bodywatching* and *Babywatching* among others
Favourite places: Many, but especially the Mediterranean and southern Europe

By the time my son Jason was one he had already travelled a great deal. I think that is one of the reasons why he was never worried by air travel. It was a bit like hopping on a bus to him, and consequently he was a very easy baby to travel with.

We lived in the Mediterranean and travelled a lot. I remember always taking a bottle of Delrosa on to the plane for him to suck, especially when the aircraft was climbing and descending. Babies' ears are extremely sensitive, especially to dramatic changes in air pressure, which is why they cry as flights come in to land or climb steeply after take-off. In my experience the people of southern Europe are more friendly and welcoming to babies than those of northern Europe.

CRAIG BROWN: Author and writer, contributor to *Private Eye* and *The Daily Telegraph* amongst other publications
Favourite place: England

It seems such a long time ago that my children were babies but I can just about remember the challenges. There probably weren't many. Silas in particular was a good baby.

Some tips I did pick up through experience. We swore by Calpol (for the children) when travelling, and earplugs so that one of us at least could sleep. Chinese and Italian restaurants seem to be the best with babies. English nappies, in my experience, don't work: buy French ones.

I remember once staying in a lovely hotel in Madrid with Silas, who was very, very young at the time but was being very good. Obviously not good enough though as, unbeknown to us, an American couple in the room next to ours had complained about him crying. We were only made aware of this one morning at reception when we went to the desk and asked for our bill to be arranged for the following day. The American woman happened to be at the desk at the same time.

'Are you going soon?' the American woman asked my wife.

'Er, yes, tomorrow,' she replied.

'Good, then we'll stay.'

My wife was rather upset about this and pushed Silas in his pushchair out of the hotel and into the streets of Madrid for a morning walk. An hour or so later she found a café and walked inside to find the American couple at one of the tables, obviously trying to escape from the noise. She smiled and sat at the table next to them, at which point Silas promptly threw a wobbly and began to cry loudly. Bless him.

TRACY EDWARDS: Round-the-world yachtswoman
Favourite place: Jordan

I'm going to make a real effort to travel as much as possible with my daughter Mackenna, as I think it's good for children to travel when they are young. I also think it will help me to see things through her eyes.

I have no idea yet how difficult it is to travel with a small child but I guess I'll find out. I may be going to Hong Kong in the near future to do a talk for the Royal Geographical Society and would like to take her with me. I won't be continuing my own travels at sea as it is too dangerous. It would be irresponsible to risk my life, now I have Mackenna to think about too.

BRIAN TURNER: Owner of Turner's restaurant in Chelsea and television celebrity cook
Favourite place: Bali

Beware of holidays which sell themselves as family friendly. Choose a holiday destination and hotel you would really like to go to, regardless of whether you have children. Ring up beforehand to see if they cater for babies. It doesn't matter where you go as long as you enjoy it and the children know you are there. Once we were on a package tour to Majorca and I knew I wouldn't like it. It was the first package tour I'd been on and my first visit to Majorca. The brochure billed it as being 'family friendly'. We were ferried around with other families and we just felt like a cog in a machine. One good thing about it though was that we were able to start up a baby-sitting circle. If you can get to know other couples, try to devise a rota so that each evening at least one couple can go out by themselves.

ALASTAIR STEWART: Presenter of London Tonight, The Sunday Programme with Alastair Stewart and Police, Camera, Action!
Favourite place: (with children) South of France, (without children) China

My wife and I are blessed with four children. My advice is to check what the children pack for a flight. Once, on a journey from Heathrow to Washington DC, we went through security and suddenly bells rang and buzzers went off. There was a terrible kerfuffle which brought Her Majesty's Constabulary running. My son Alexander had packed a perfect replica of a revolver amongst his Snoopy books and other favourite things without us realising.

He was seriously told off which we thought was a bit heavy. They then confiscated the 'gun', packed it into a jiffy bag sealed with black and yellow striped tape, and it was carried as 'special luggage'. When we arrived in Washington DC, it was returned to us.

Family holidays are important to us. You are buying precious time when you can be a unit. The venue more often than not is a big house with a swimming pool, but not too far from a beach. This is better for us than hotels which become very expensive for six. The place we like the best is in the hills looking down on St Tropez, in the middle of a vineyard. There is a couple who look after us to make sure we don't stray off the beaten track.

It is a great shame that business class travel is so expensive, as a child's car seat fits perfectly into a business class seat. I suggest you save up, don't fly as often, but fly well when you do. You can't do that in economy class. Never, ever have a baby on your lap – find the money to pay for the extra seat. If a booking is made at the same time for six people, say three adults and three children, you would think it quite likely that they would like to sit together, especially with babies and children. But often this doesn't seem to register with the booking clerk. Families deserve to travel together, so ask even if they think you are being difficult.

MAUREEN LIPMAN: Actress and author
Favourite places: Cork, Ireland and New York

As babies, my children were better travellers than I was, or am. My brother Geoffrey Lipman is a world expert in tourism. He is permanently jet-lagged but he loves it and I'm such a Taurean, I just love being in my home. Disaster seems to dog me on my travels. We had a typhoon in Boston, forest fires in South Africa and an earthquake in California when I was there. But I've had great holidays in Ireland and Cornwall.

British Airways are good with babies. When we were recently flying from South Africa, there were two babies travelling with their parents in the seats in front of us, and the stewardesses were absolutely fantastic. Ferrying them about, looking after them. You could hardly tell they were there.

My kids always had a wonderful inner life, and found ways to entertain themselves. You don't need to carry a huge case of fluffy toys with you wherever you go. All mine seemed to want when we were flying was their sleep – and me, of course.

LORRAINE KELLY: Presenter on GMTV
Favourite places: USA, Alaska, Far East

Before we had Rosie we were much more adventurous, visiting China and the Far East. But with a baby you go where they have good healthcare. Most people dread the long plane journey. I always used to ask for a bassinet, because if you have to sit in your seat for five to nine hours it is not a good idea to have the baby on your lap even if she is very small. I always take a bag now with little toys which I wrap up. Rosie is five now and she is a very good traveller, but there is a fine line between a cute child and an annoying one. Ours likes to help the cabin staff. She was about six weeks old when she first went to Scotland, and now she wants to be an air hostess when she grows up! She loves the whole idea of travelling.

When I was five, I went on a ferry down the Clyde. When I ask Rosie where she would like to go to this year she always says New York or Singapore. It is a completely different world.

ANNABEL KARMEL: Author and expert on children's food
Favourite place: Courcheval, France

When travelling with a baby, fruits like banana, avocado and papaya make great portable instant baby food. All you will need is a knife to peel them and a fork to mash them with, so you don't need to rely exclusively on jars and packets.

One of the most embarrassing moments in my travels with a baby occurred when we were in a restaurant in France. We travelled everywhere with a folding portable high chair for my then one-year-old that clipped onto the side of a table. Everything was great and we were all very hungry and looking forward to a slap-up lunch. Unfortunately, the table to which we had clipped the high chair was a little unstable. No sooner had the waiter brought our food than my son started wriggling and the whole table came crashing down – leaving plates, glasses, food and a pretty terrified Nicholas on the floor. I scooped him up in my arms and rushed outside leaving behind a horrible mess and a very irate French proprietor.

JACK HIGGINS: Best-selling novelist
Favourite place: The Caribbean, especially St John's and St Thomas in the British Virgin Islands

We travelled everywhere with our children when they were very young. Definitely the easiest time to do this is in the first year. I was very surprised by how people react to breast-feeding in different countries. It's the most natural thing in the world but in some countries people are so sensitive about it. What I also found surprising is the lack of sympathy you can find on planes amongst both cabin crew and other passengers. Take the toilets, for example. There is only just about enough room for one person. We have had many interesting experiences changing babies while they have been balanced across our knees. Other passengers would look at us when we entered the toilet as though we were completely mad. But what else are you supposed to do – change the baby in front of everyone? Now that would cause concern.

PATRICIA WILLIAMSON: Producer and presenter of various travel shows on television, including LWT's Dream Ticket
Favourite places: India and the Caribbean

I've had good experiences and bad experiences when travelling with my two boys as babies. First the bad one. A Caribbean holiday was not the greatest for Dominic. Eleven years ago, baby Dom got a tummy bug that needed treatment, an ear infection that also involved trips to the doctor, and was paranoid about beaches – he just wouldn't go near the sand. Wild horses wouldn't keep him away now.

His younger brother Edward was a different story. At the same age he thrived in the Caribbean and posed no problems on two skiing trips either. He is, I hasten to add, built like a Tonka toy.

I think what this says is that travelling with children has more to do with the child than the destination. Some babies can take more than others, so 'know your child' must be rule number one. Heat, new food, new people, ability to cope with long journeys and new environments and disrupted sleep patterns must all be taken into consideration. Of course, there are always those tricky little characters who surprise everyone either way … Perhaps I should expand rule number one to 'know your child but be prepared for surprises'!

JUDITH CHALMERS: Presenter of ITV's Wish You Were Here?
Favourite place: The Algarve

Neil and I have always enjoyed travelling with our children and now with our grandchildren as well. The airlines are much more geared up to young babies than they were 20 years ago. There are mother and baby facilities in the airports and on the planes; including cots for very young babies. A great number of destinations across the world now cater for children. Many of the large hotels have nanny facilities and baby minding and even crèches which means that all the family can have a holiday. Our family holidays are spent on The Algarve in Portugal where there are long stretches of excellent beaches beside the Atlantic. One thing you need to be very careful of, though, in sunny parts of the world, is sunburn. Protective creams are a *must*. Choose a destination you want to go to first and then check if the hotel and airline can fully cater for your baby.

LAURENCE LLEWELYN BOWEN: Interior designer and resident designer on Changing Rooms
Favourite place: Cornwall

Both our children are good travellers and we travelled extensively with them when they were very young. A trunkful of Calpol is always useful when they are small, of course. We took Cecile to Paris when she was only a couple of weeks old. The Eurostar was great but on this particular occasion we had left the baby bag behind (the one you can't do without) and couldn't get back through the barriers to collect it. The train was held up anyway, and as we were waiting for the bag to be delivered down the platform all these Chinese whispers crept through the train as people were being told Laurence Llewelyn Bowen had left his baby behind on the platform! Did I get some funny looks ...

ALASTAIR McKENZIE: Managing Editor, Travel News Organisation
Favourite place: BC (before child) – Tongabezi, Zambia: AD (after little darling) – Smugglers Notch, Vermont, USA

As everybody says, the best age to take children abroad and especially on long flights, is when they are too young to require an expensive seat (under two) and before they can walk (because they want to get up and walk all over the aeroplane every ten minutes). So we took our son Joe as far as we could when he was 13 months old – to New Zealand! On the whole it worked out very well. On the way out we stopped off in Singapore for a couple of days to give him a chance to acclimatise and reset his body clock before setting off again. But on the return journey we thought we would just get it all over with in one long 35-hour marathon (we had to change planes in Sydney and stopover in Singapore). Joe was very good really. There were long periods when he required lots of attention, but somewhere over Afghanistan he settled down to sleep in his bassinet. (If your child is young enough these are wonderful things; bulkhead-mounted cots. Make sure you order one well in advance.) He woke up about an hour before we landed. My memory of that flight is of the moment about 40 minutes from landing when Sophie and I were lying stretched-out, semi-conscious, exhausted and surrounded by debris. In the aisle on both sides of us were the usual pre-landing queues for the toilets ...

being entertained by my now wide-awake son, who was sitting in his bassinet with a pair of headphones on, waving his arms about to the music and shrieking with laughter!

SIMON BEECHING: Managing Director, WEXAS International, The Independent Traveller's Club, www.wexas.com
Favourite place: St Mawes in Cornwall, the most relaxing place on earth – 'my cottage or the terrace of the Tresanton Hotel'

Pre-book a bassinet well in advance, so you don't have to carry your baby on your lap, especially when they're nearly two – the bassinet is still big enough to sleep in. If you have a choice of destination, fly North–South (Africa, Mediterranean, Indian Ocean) especially where there are night flights. This avoids jet lag and any loss of sleep rhythm. It's nicer travelling with a sleeping baby than one that's awake. Carry a pack with enough food and drink for the baby for 24 hours, so if there's a delay and you are stuck somewhere, you don't have a screaming, hungry, dirty infant. Make sure you have all you are likely to need in your hand luggage, especially nappies, formula, sterilised bottles and juice.

We arrived in Bangkok once at 2am but our luggage went on to Taipei. Two babies to change – and the nappies in Taipei! An hour spent looking for a late-night shop near the airport with a fractious family is not funny after a long-haul flight. Still, success smelt sweet, literally. Babies love sitting near the big screen video and will sit up mesmerised (and quiet) at the moving colours on-screen. Make sure an infant has a dummy to suck or a bottle on take-off or landing, it stops their ears hurting and they don't cry.

JOHN CARTER: Former presenter of the Holiday Programme and Wish You Were Here?
Favourite place: Different places for different reasons

We took our three children on a cruise many years ago, when we were too inexperienced to listen to the prophecies of doom from all sides. It was tremendous – no child fell overboard, was seasick or became lost in a foreign port. On the contrary, they and other junior passengers were taken under the professional wings of the nursery staff, played to their heart's content and were spoiled rotten.

They ate breakfast and lunch with us – discovering that a small child could go round the deck buffet several times without fear of challenge – and had their 'high tea' with other children in plenty of time to be bedded (or, rather, bunked) down before 'grown-up dinner'.

All this food was clearly insufficient because one afternoon we encountered the children carrying large slabs of chocolate, purchased from the ship's shop.

How? They had been given no pocket money (on board they had no need of it), and the possibility of earning it from, say, a paper round, was not high.

The answer came quickly. Our three, and most of the other children on board, had spent a morning in the nursery drawing pictures. After lunch they had prowled the deck, offering their pictures to recumbent adults. Disinclined to spurn such offers, the elderly passengers were completely taken aback when the little angels said: 'That will be two pence, please.'

I had a shrewd idea which child was behind this little enterprise, so spent a lot of time apologising. Our fellow passengers took it in good part, telling tales about their own grandchildren and producing cherished photographs.

Any lingering social ice was well and truly broken. That evening the grown-ups had the best party of the whole trip. Thankfully, the children slept through it all.

USEFUL INFORMATION

REFERENCE SECTION

The opinions expressed in *Have Baby Will Travel* are subjective not objective. There are other books which list hotels to stay in and airlines to travel with and what they cost. My reference section includes only details of those airlines, airports, train companies, ferries, resorts and hotels, and tour operators that I have personally experienced. This is a personal choice – and your experience may differ. I found those I have listed to be helpful and friendly and in general they made travelling with Tom a pleasure.

Travelling with a baby is a very individual experience. The ease with which you do so depends less on the facilities and more on the helpfulness of those around you and their attitude to you. Above all, your own attitude as a mother is vitally important – and, lest I forget, the father too.

Just because a hotel says it welcomes babies doesn't guarantee the receptionist on the day will give you a welcoming smile. Nor that the changing room at the station will be clean or available when you need it. Nor that the train will run on time, or – indeed – that your baby will sleep or smile throughout the journey.

So when can you start to travel with your baby? The National Childbirth Trust recommends that a new baby should not fly until the alveoli in their lungs are fully expanded, which would generally be at one week old. If a baby was premature or it had a respiratory infection or condition it might need extra oxygen when flying. A really young baby would probably be more comfortable if it was fed during take off and landing. It would be as well to check with a doctor that a very young baby was fit to fly. There was a suggestion of a link between cot death and flying in the press in March 1998, but this link has not been proven.

AIRPORTS

The best airport I have travelled to or from with Tom is Stansted. The worst was Charles De Gaulle in Paris (confusing, no signs, no facilities that I could find). Here is a brief summary of the main airports in the UK and my experiences of them.

Heathrow

There are baby care rooms air and landside (i.e. before and after passport control) in all four terminals, changing facilities in both piers and in landside catering areas. The airport information guide indicates where these are. There are no facilities for heating bottles and food in these areas but food areas in Terminal One such as Garfunkel's restaurant (also offers goody bags, high chairs, bottle and babyfood warming); Harry Ramsden's (high chairs and warming); Café One (goody bags, high chairs and warming); and Burger King Express (high chairs and bottle warming) should be able to help.

If you are travelling with a child of the opposite sex to yourself and need to take them to the toilet there are unisex accessible toilets.

There are no play areas designed for young passengers boarding through the UK though there is an unsupervised children's play area on the middle floor of the Flight Connections Centre with climbing frame and soft toys. There are plans to upgrade the play facilities in the babycare areas. Parents travelling alone with young children receive help from Skycaps porters at the airport.

The changing rooms are clean and easy to find.

Gatwick

Gatwick offers specially equipped rooms for feeding and changing babies, indicated by either a bottle sign or a baby care symbol. Other changing facilities are provided en route to the departure gates, in the transfer area and after passport control on arrival. Fold-down tables are provided in some ladies' and gentlemen's toilets.

A number include bottle-warming facilities and two changing rooms have also been adapted to provided facilities for disabled parents. There is a play area on the landside in the South Terminal and airside in the North Terminal including soft play areas, slides and cartoons.

The changing rooms are clean and easy to find.

Stansted

Unisex baby care rooms are indicated by the NCT symbol. Equipped with nappy dispensers, changing tables and areas for feeding. There are some in the main terminal and Satellite One. One catering outlet will provide hot water to heat baby food. There is a children's play area in the international departure lounge and a play table is available in each satellite building. There are air fun entertainment centres throughout the terminal and Satellite One includes games for all age-groups. Changing rooms are clean and easy to find.

City

City offers a baby changing room next to the ladies' toilet on the ground floor. The coffee shop and brasserie restaurant landside and the airside restaurant bar could help heat a baby bottle. Changing room easy to find.

Luton

There is a baby care room both on the check-in concourse and in the departure lounge, with changing tables and nappy dispenser. All food outlets will heat a baby bottle and provide baby food, though only KFC outlet landside offers a child's menu. Airtours has sponsored an unsupervised play centre in the international departure lounge for children from 2 to 8 years. Changing room clean and easy to find.

MAJOR AIRLINES

Most airlines fly babies under 2 years for 10% of the adult fare. Some offer a full range of facilities while others have only a limited service. Although Air France don't offer baby food, I really liked their approach with Tom when I flew with them. Air France is the runner-up to Emirates, who win for staff friendliness and overall service.

Air France
Air France does not offer baby food, and the meal must be provided by the parents. However, should the parent have forgotten or run out of food, the airline does provide infant milk, baby food, bottled water and baby bottles in limited quantities. A carrycot is provided that clips on the bulkhead, but due to its size (70 cm long) it is only suitable for the very young (up to one year). They are in soft fabric, with pillows and blankets provided. A baby cot should be requested when making your booking (or 24 hours before departure at the latest).

On long-haul flights, parents with babies are the first to board. Buggies are put in the hold, especially on European narrow-bodied aircraft. They are delivered to the arrival baggage carousel. Washing and changing your baby is possible, as there are changing tables on all Air France long haul flights. Moreover, the flight attendant will give mothers a baby's travel kit with a small teddy bear, paper tissues, eau de toilette and bib, and is on hand to help mothers at mealtimes.

Infants pay 10% of the applicable fare except in mainland France, where they travel free. International journeys inside the area USA-Canada-Mexico, St Domingo, Cuba, Haiti, Jamaica and the Bahamas are also free. Excellent.

Air New Zealand
Babies are charged 10% of adult fare. Baby food provided if pre-booked, and milk will be heated. Cots are available if pre-booked, and staff trained in first aid. Very friendly and Tom was offered a teddy and a goody bag.

British Airways
You pay 10% of the adult fare but no seat is offered up to 2 years. If your child requires a seat, you pay for a child ticket at the rate of 62% of the adult fare. There is limited availability of baby food or you can

take your own and staff will heat it up. Changing facilities are limited on the smaller planes used for shorter journeys. There are cots only on long-haul flights and these need to be booked well in advance. Staff are trained to deal with babies and all are trained in first aid. Very friendly and helpful. BA has recently installed a luxury carry cot on their Boeing 747s, 767s and 777s for long-haul flights. Designed for babies of up to six months, they enable the baby to lie completely flat in the carry cot attached to a bulkhead in the aircraft. Over 60,000 infants are carried by BA during a single year and the cots will be available in all classes, booked in advance on a first come, first served basis. They cannot, however, be used during turbulence.

Continental Airlines
Continental offers 165 destinations in North, Latin and South America and has a codeshare with Virgin on the same routes. They have baby-changing facilities on all planes and kiddie bags on board. Very friendly.

Emirates
Costs 10% of adult fare and cots are provided. Staff are trained in baby care. Baby food is provided if booked in advance and milk can be heated. If you ask for organic baby food in advance, they will order it for you. There is lots of space, even in economy. Emirates also has specially trained baby care cabin crew, who assist parents with very young babies and infants. On board, they carry baby kits, which include nappies, baby bibs, feeding bottles, and talcum powder. They also offer soft toys to babies and infants. Excellent.

Iberia
Baby food is supplied if requested. Cots are not available on short-haul flights, but are on long-haul flights on B747, DC10 and Airbus 340. Cots are permitted for infants up to the age of 8 months. Iberia provides a baby care kit to make the trip more comfortable on long-haul flights. Baby pays 10% of adult fare.

Jersey European Airways
Children under 2 years accompanied by an adult and not occupying a seat travel free. Jersey European Airlines provides an advice booklet for how to travel with young children. Baby changing facilities available on plane. Very friendly.

Lauda Air

Lauda Air will provide baby food in flight if notified 24 hours before departure. Organic baby food is not served as standard. Special bassinet cots are available on all flights, again with 24-hour notice. Mothers with babies are the only travellers permitted to pre-book the bulkhead seats which offer the most leg room. Lauda Air is primarily a leisure travel airline and welcomes families with babies and children on board. Children aged between 2–12 years receive a Niki's Kids Club pack on board while the in-flight entertainment system offers cartoons and the Niki's Kids Club music channel. There is no restriction on babies travelling in business class (Lauda has no first class). For both economy and business class tickets, babies (aged 1 day to 2 years) pay 10% of adult fare. Very helpful and friendly.

Malaysia Airlines

Malaysia Airlines do offer baby food, including organic, but a request for this must be made at least 24 hours in advance. They also offer nappies, sterilised bottles and milk and charge 10% of the published fare for the baby's flight. They have a number of baby cots on board. As these are located at bulkheads, they are offered with pre-assigned seats, and where possible, these seats are kept for parents with babies. Request this seat/baby cot when making the booking for the flight, as they are assigned on a first come-first served basis. Very helpful.

Monarch Airlines

Heinz baby food is offered on board. Babies pay 10% of adult fare plus tax. All special requests for cots and food should be made at time of reservation. Cots can be provided only if two passengers are travelling with the infant.

Qantas

Babies are charged at 10% of adult fare – no seat. Baby food is available but not organic; you can take your own. Changing facilities are in all the toilets. Cots are provided but not guaranteed. These need to be booked and availability depends on when the booking is made. Early booking is recommended (i.e. more than a week in advance). All staff are trained to deal with babies. Very friendly.

Singapore Airlines

Babies travel at 10% of the normal adult fare, aged 1 day to 2 years. Baby food is supplied if given 24 hours notice, but it is not organic. They have changing facilities in one or two of their toilets on the plane. They offer cots which are screwed into the wall, which must be booked at more than 24 hours' notice. All staff are fully trained to deal with babies and a mother would not be refused entry to business or first class if travelling with a baby. Very friendly. Lots of space on economy.

Thai Airways

There are ticket concessions for up to 2 years of age, at 10% of the adult fare. However, the child is not entitled to a seat. Baby food is available but it is not organic. There is at least one changing room facility available. Very friendly.

Virgin Atlantic Airways

There are ticket concessions depending on where you travel and for how long and when. No baby food supplied, organic or otherwise. There are changing facilities in all the toilets on board the plane. Virgin offers 'sky cots' which are only for certain seats so you need to book well in advance. Staff are trained to deal with babies on board including from a health and safety viewpoint. Very friendly.

Some useful airline websites and reservation numbers:

Aer Lingus	www.aerlingus.ie	020 8899 4747
Aerolineas Argentinas	www.aerolineas.com.ar	020 7494 1001
Air Canada	www.aircanada.ca	0990 247226
Air France	www.airfrance.com	020 8742 6600
Air Malta	www.airmalta.com	020 7292 4949
Air Mauritius	www.airmauritius.com	020 7434 4375
Air New Zealand	www.airnz.co.uk	020 8741 2299
Air Seychelles		01293 529429
Air 2000	www.air2000.co.uk	0161 745 4644
Alitalia	www.alitalia.co.uk	020 7602 7111
All Nippon Airways	www.ana-europe.com	0345 262 262
American Airlines	www.aa.com	020 8572 5555
Austrian Airlines	www.aua.com	0845 6010948
Britannia Airways	www.britanniaairways.com	

British Airways	www.british-airways.com	0345 222111
British Midland	www.britishmidland.com	0345 554554
Buzz	www.buzzaway.com	0870 2407070
BWIA	www.bwee.com	020 8577 1100
Cathay Pacific	www.cathaypacific.com	020 7747 8888
Continental Airlines	www.continental.com	01293 776464
Delta Airlines	www.delta-air.com	0800 414767
Eastern Airways	www.easternairways.co.uk	01652 680600
easyJet	www.easyjet.com	0870 6000000
Egyptair	www.egyptair.com.eg	020 7734 5864
El Al Israel Airlines	www.elal.co.il	020 7437 9255
Emirates	www.emirates.com	020 7808 0808
Finnair	www.finnair.fi	020 7408 1222
Go	www.go-fly.com	01279 666388
Gulf Air	www.gulfairco.com	020 7408 1717
Iberia	www.iberia.com	020 7830 0011
Icelandair	www.icelandair.co.uk	020 7388 5599
Japan Air Lines	www.japanair.com	0345 747700
Jersey European	www.jersey-european.co.uk	0990 676676
KLM - UK	www.klmuk.com	0870 5074074
KLM	www.klm.com	0990 750900
Lauda Air	www.laudaair.com	0845 6010934
Lufthansa	www.lufthansa.co.uk	0345 737747
Luxair	www.luxair.lu	020 8745 4254
Maersk Air	www.british-airways.com	020 7333 0066
Malaysia Airlines	www.malaysia-airlines.com.my	020 7341 2020
Manx Airlines	www.manx-airlines.com	0345 256256
Meridiana	www.meridiana.it	020 7839 2222
Monarch Airlines	www.monarch-airlines.com	01582 398333
Northwest Airlines	www.nwa.com	0990 561000
Olympic Airways	www.olympic-airways.gr	020 7409 3400
Qantas Airways	www.qantas.com.au	0345 747767
Qatar Airways	www.qatarairways.com	020 7896 3636
Royal Air Maroc		020 7439 4361
Royal Brunei Airlines		020 7584 6660
Royal Jordanian		020 7878 6333
Ryanair	www.ryanair.com	0541 569 569
Sabena	www.sabena.com	0845 601 0933
SAS	www.flysas.co.uk	020 8990 7122

Singapore Airlines	www.singaporeair.com	020 8747 0007
South African Airways		0870 747 1111
Spanair	www.spanair.com	01293 516229
SriLankan Airlines	www.airlanka.com	020 7930 4688
Suckling Airways		0870 6060707
Swissair	www.swissair.com	0845 601 0956
TAP Air Portugal	www.tap-airportugal.tp	0845 601 0932
Thai Airways	www.thaiair.com	020 7499 9113
Trans World Airlines	www.twa.com	0345 33 33 33
Turkish Airlines		0845 601 0931
Tyrolean Airlines		0845 601 0948
United Airlines	www.ual.com	0845 8444777
US Airways	www.usairways.com	0800 7835556
Varig		020 7287 3131
Virgin Atlantic Airways	www.fly.virgin.com	01293 747747
Virgin Express	www.virgin-express.com	020 7744 0004
VLM Flemish Airlines	www.vlm-air.com	020 7476 6677

Information supplied by the Travel News Organisation
www.travel-news.org

TOUR OPERATORS

If you don't want to go it alone and want to be packaged ...There are dozens of tour operators out there who offer excellent facilities for babies. Club Med are particularly good. Most of the mainstream tour operators offer a good range of facilities from cots to baby minding services. I have only taken one package to date with Tom – and my experience with First Choice was a good one.

Skiing holidays

First Choice Ski offers a crèche for infants aged from 6 months up to 3 years. This facility is available in the following ski resorts: Les Deux Alpes, Alpe D'Huez and Les Menuires. In order to allow parents to spend more time with their children, First Choice Ski has a flexible programme allowing you to choose the amount of child care which suits you best.

There are designated crèche areas within First Choice Ski hotels equipped with toys and games. These are staffed by NNEB (or equivalent) trained nannies. A strict ratio of one nanny to three children is maintained in all crèches. Activities take place indoors and out depending on the weather. Lunch is not included and parents should provide food/bottles/nappies etc. for infants under 2 years. Lunch can be arranged locally for children over 2 for a small supplement.

Another ski company targeting families with babies is Powder Byrne. They have crèches in all their resorts catering for an age range from 6 months to 4 years old (this compares with some crèches in Canada which take babies from 4 weeks). Each crèche is headed by an English-speaking, fully qualified nanny. They are open five days a week (Monday-Friday) and operate from 09.30 to 16.30. Children's places must be reserved at the time of booking and you may then use the service as often as you like. The world's largest toy store, Hamley's, is now teaming up with Powder Byrne to provide equipment for its children's clubs. They have a website at www.powderbyrne.com and their e-mail address is enquiries@powderbyrne.co.uk.

Airfares

A flat rate charge is made for infants under 2 years of age travelling by charter flight and a higher one on a scheduled flight. If travelling by air, infants must sit on an adult's lap. There is no baggage allowance for infants, although a collapsible pushchair may be carried free of charge. Hoteliers may charge a supplement locally for infants. This may be in addition to the cost for cots and infant food, and varies from hotel to hotel.

Villa packs

First Choice and Sovereign offer villa baby packs. These can be booked before departure and will be waiting on arrival at the villa. They will include a cot, a highchair and a buggy with sun canopy. Avent Naturally provide a bottle warmer and a bottle steriliser. These villa packs are offered in all villas and apartments in Majorca, Menorca, Fuerteventura and the Algarve and the cost varies according to length of stay. Cots alone can also be pre-booked for a specific charge.

TRAIN OPERATORS

My view on travelling by train in the UK with Tom is tarnished by my poor experiences – not so much because of the trains, but because of the other passengers on them. However, the best experiences and services seem to be on Virgin (which won an award for their friendliness to families last year), and Eurostar – if you can find a space in the relevant carriage. Virgin, I am informed, are improving their baby facilities. Eurostar service and facilities are impeccable.

Connex
Under 5s travel free. No baby food is available. There are buffet facilities on most of the services and baby food can be heated up there. On trains without a buffet a trolley service is provided, which would be able to offer hot water to stand food in. No changing facilities on board at the moment. We were told it would be OK to change your baby on a table provided that this did not cause offence to other passengers. (If I was another passenger, it would.) I wouldn't have dreamt of changing Tom on any of the Connex trains.

Eurostar
Under 4s travel free. No baby food is provided but your own food can be heated. There are two family coaches, with changing rooms situated between them. You need to request in advance to be seated near these when you book. Coaches 17 and 2 have changing facilities and family coaches are 1 and 18, which are only available at the weekend. Staff are trained in first aid but not specifically in how to handle babies. Travelling on Eurostar was a brilliant experience.

Eurotunnel
At both Calais and Folkestone the passenger terminals offer baby care facilities.

First Great Western
First Great Western has baby changing facilities on all of its services, which operate between London Paddington and South Wales, the West Country and the Cotswolds. The on-train facilities are in Coach E. At weekends and during school holidays Coach E is the Family Carriage and is set aside for mums, dads and children. There is

seating and space for pushchairs. Free activity packs are available for children. Seats can be reserved in advance by telephoning 0845 700 0125.

Infants travel free. No baby food is provided but they are willing to heat a bottle and food in a microwave provided it is already covered with clingfilm. Changing facilities are available in Coach E next to the buffet car. There are no plans to introduce baby food on to the menu and staff are not trained to deal with babies.

South West Trains

Infants travel free up to age 5. Baby food is not available and can only be heated at the discretion of the buffet manager. This would probably depend on how busy they were. There are changing facilities on the Weymouth lines only, but they are in the process of introducing changing facilities on all the West of England and Exeter lines. These will continue to be introduced on other trains. Staff are not trained specifically to deal with babies but they all know basic first aid and have mobile phones should anything 'serious' happen.

Virgin

Virgin have installed baby changing facilities on some of the trains they inherited from British Rail. The new fleet scheduled to run in 2001 will all have baby changing facilities. Virgin offer a system of booking assistance called JourneyCare on 0345 443366, which enables customers to arrange to be met and assisted to board/detrain at either end of their journey. JourneyCare is available for all sorts of people, from the elderly to those with babies and toddlers. Virgin's station staff are encouraged to assist people as much as possible whether the customer has booked JourneyCare or not. Last year, Virgin Trains won a 1999 Parent Friendly Public Transport Award (sponsored by Huggies) in the Tommy's Campaign for the 1999 Parent Friendly Award. Parents throughout the UK nominated them for a number of reasons including 'the friendly service by their people'.

No baby food is available but they are willing to heat food up provided it is in a suitable container.

LONDON CAB FIRMS

Computer Cabs – London
All the new cabs have built-in baby seats. You need to request one when making a booking. Most cabbies are brilliant with babies and each of them has his own story to tell. Most will help you and your baby out of the cab – unless you get a particularly grumpy one.

Just Airports Taxis
Can supply child seats at £4 per seat on trips to and from London airports. One of the new black cab models now includes an integral child seat.

CAR RENTAL WEBSITES AND PHONE NUMBERS

Alamo	www.goalamo.com	0990 994000
Autos Abroad		020 7409 1900
Avis	www.avis.com	0990 900500
Budget Rent-a-Car	www.budget.com	01541 565656
Dollar Rent-a-Car		0800 252897
Europcar	www.europcar.com	0870 6075000
Executive Car Rental	www.etclub.com	0990 133056
Gold Medal		0870 6063001
Guy Salmon		0870 6043800
Hertz	www.hertz.com	0990 996699
Holiday Autos	www.holidayautos.co.uk	0990 300400
National	www.nationalcar.co.uk	0870 6006666
Pelican Car Hire		01625 586666
Premier Car Hire		01279 641040
Sixt		0845 600 6660
Speciality Auto Rentals		020 8876 9286
Suncars		0870 5005566
Thrifty	www.thrifty.co.uk	0990 168238

Information supplied by the Travel News Organisation
www.travel-news.org

RESTAURANT CHAINS IN THE UK

Restaurant chains which are geared for children are of course the American and American-style fast food ones, McDonald's and its clones. In the UK Pizza Express is a preferable alternative as is Café Rouge, and especially if you go when they are not absolutely packed. Harvester consistently gets the vote as the most family friendly of the big chains and you should also be safe with the Little Chef – if uninspired by the grown-up menu yourself. On the other hand, if you invest in *The Good Pub Guide* and/or *The CAMRA Guide to Family Pubs* you should be able to eat in more convivial surroundings which are also reasonably child-friendly. *The Good Pub Guide* has a section on pubs with good gardens, which are obviously the ones to pick for children if the weather is fine.

USEFUL PUBLICATION

If you subscribe to only one publication subscribe to this one: Kate Calvert's *Family Travel*, a quarterly publication on different destinations and types of holidays with children. She doesn't just focus on babies. It is a bible of where to go and where not to go. To subscribe send a cheque for £14.95 payable to Family Travel at 1 Hargrave Road, London N19 5SH. A sample issue is £5 with £9.95 being the cost of upgrading to the full year. For more details visit http://www.family-travel.co.uk or phone 020 7272 7441.

THE INTERNET

I asked David Winder, associate editor of *PC Pro Magazine* (who has recently written a book on using the internet for travel reservations) for his advice on finding baby-friendly destinations. This is what he told me.

What sites exist for those who wish to travel with babies and children which are good – which ones would you recommend?

I'd recommend firstly trying the specialist travel related search engines and directories, as you can then search specifically for keywords such as children, family, or baby facilities for example. The Virgin Internet Travel Guide lists a number of such websites in a chapter devoted to finding travel-related resources on the web. However, my favourite recommendations would be:

AltaVista TravelZone
http://search.thetrip.com

Lycos UK Travel
http://www.lycos.co.uk/webguides/travel

Virgin Net Travel
http://www.virgin.net/travel

Yahoo Travel
http://travel.yahoo.com

Are there any good sites and, if so, which are the quickest and easiest to use if you have a young family?

There are literally hundreds of 'good' sites, but these will be different for every person who uses the web. Your own criteria will vary from those of the next person, or even the next young family.

Some idea of what you want to get from a browsing expedition on the web is a good idea before getting connected. I tend to jot down a list of things I want to do and then stick to that – it is all too easy to get distracted by irrelevance and then find you've spent two hours buying books at Amazon or downloading MP3 music files by some obscure African brass band, and not actually done any of the things you really wanted to do!

Some sites which spring to mind as being useful for family travel, by my personal criteria at least, include:

Travel Health Online
http://www.tripprep.com

Cuts, Bites and Stings (First Aid For Travellers)
http://www.lonelyplanet.com/health/cuts.htm

Travel Library
http://www.travel-library.com

EmbassyWeb
http://www.embpage.org

****

In my experience there are two other general sites that you will also find useful:

ABTA
http://www.abtanet.com
While ABTA may not know everything about babies they are linked to all their members' sites and a visit to the ABTA website is a good way to check up on the comapny with whom you are thinking of booking.

Travelleronline
http://www.travelleronline.com
This site provides information on all types of travel, including travel with children and travel health. The site is run by WEXAS Travel Club, publishers of *Traveller* magazine, *The Traveller's Handbook* and *The Traveller's Healthbook*. The site also provides a wealth of other travel links and online travel-planning tools, plus cheap annual travel insurance (children are covered free) and a chat forum.

ONLINE TRAVEL AGENCIES

The internet is constantly changing but here are some of the current sites, at the time of going to press, that you might like to visit.

airline-network.co.uk
Refreshingly simple and quick site to use. The fares it comes up with are not bad either.

deckchair.com
Bob Geldof's simple-to-use online flight agency. It was launched in spring 1999 promising to do just one thing really well; make it easy to find and book the lowest airline fares. Its immediate popularity made it slow and prone to crashing in the early days. Now it does offer some of the lowest fares most of the time, although it still has occasional technical problems.

ebookers.com
This is the innovatory online service of Flightbookers, one of the major fares consolidators. It also has a couple of clever services; Fare Alert, where customers can identify a destination and date, and are then notified when the fare drops below their specified threshold price, and Bid & Go, an auction area where customers give a fare limit to a given destination and ebookers.com try to find an airline willing to accept it.

eDreams.com
An American startup (March 1999) based in Silicon Valley but selling package holidays to European consumers. This site is in its early stages. It is a 'department store' site, offering tour operators the chance to sell their holidays online through the eDreams site, on which eDreams then take commission. Visitors enter search criteria and are led to the most suitable holidays. It also offers DreamGuides – online travel experts who can answer specific queries about where to go and what to do.

escaperoutes.com
The latest travel site from EMAP (See A2B and BargainHolidays). This site concentrates on holiday packages, as well as offering other

components and info, features and tips. It has a simple approach and is very good for browsing. It has Email News and Offers – weekly updates on exclusive travel offers, last-minute deals, great getaways and Traveller's Tales – where you can join fellow travellers in online chat, share great discoveries, holiday nightmares and more.

expedia.com

The first major eAgency. It was launched by Microsoft in the US first as Expedia.com and for a couple of years we in the UK could only look at all the cheap flights and travel components, but couldn't buy. Eventually they created this UK version. It is comprehensive (published and discounted fares on over 450 airlines, a directory of 40,000 hotels worldwide, car hire from more than 40 rental companies and a choice of 75,000 package holidays) if not always the cheapest. Its most irritating feature used to be the need to register your details before it would look up a fare for you. This has at long last been rectified. The site also includes in-depth destination guides and maps, a travel information service with an online magazine, and links to relevant websites. It is updated every 30 minutes.

holidayextras.com

A new website offering online booking for a range of UK airport based holiday extras like airport hotels, car parks, lounges and transfers, plus foreign exchange and travel insurance. For example you can check availability and book space at airport car parks. It is operated by ABC Holiday Extras who, since 1983, have been wholesalers dealing in UK airport hotels and car parks for the retail travel trade.

hotelnet.com

Accommodation-only agency for hotels throughout Europe, USA, Canada and South Africa. It acts as an agency for only a handful of clients (e.g. Johansons, Choice, Minôtel, Relais & Chateaux) so the choices can be a bit limited.

lastminute.com

Famous home of late-availability holidays. If you are looking for excellent bargains and really can drop everything and go at a moment's notice, this is the place to look. They used to concentrate on flight deals but they've now expanded into accommodation offers as well.

qxl.com
QXL is the well-known UK online auction house. Rather like lastminute.com, this is the place to find excellent bargains. The travel section regularly auctions off spare capacity from the major tour operators and airlines, so if you want stay in a 4-star hotel in the Caribbean next week for three hundred quid … start here!

spaceonline.com
Going Places' incredibly stylish online flight-only site. Some of the fares are very good indeed, but there are not enough of them and all that style comes with a big speed penalty. Navigation around the site is pretty easy but in the end, you are left with a 24-hour phone line to call if you want to book or check something out.

Teletext
The old workhorse of electronic distribution has a new face, and all those cheap holidays (20,000 of them) you used to find in block graphics on your telly, you will soon be able to find and book on your computer. In the meantime you are being directed to the telephone booking services of its advertisers.

travelocity.com
Back in the early 1970s a smart guy (called Max Hopper) working for American Airlines realised that there was no reason why travel agents couldn't key in reservations themselves if they were connected to the same computer the AA reservations department used. Thus started SABRE, the first Computer Reservation System. It is now used globally by hundreds of thousands of travel agents booking flights, hotels and cars from all the major companies. Travelocity is SABRE on the internet, the same system the professionals use.

travelstore.com
Started out in July 1999 as Eclipsis.com but quickly changed its name to travelstore. The first eAgency to be accepted into the ranks of ABTA. It is now aimed firmly at business travellers and frequent flyers, who are typically self-employed or work for small to medium sized enterprises. It offers flights on 532 airlines and rooms at 40,000 hotels.

The site has recently been redesigned (January 2000) and it is busy developing sophisticated corporate travel management systems and facilities. In February it bought out one of its main competitors, Equator-net.

trrravel.com

A new kid on the block. We are not sure what their pedigree is (we suspect they may be related to a well-known discount fares agency in Alton, Hampshire). They claim to be, wait for it, 'a one-stop online travel service that promises to change the way consumers buy holidays flights and book hotels'... so nothing special there.

uTravel.co.uk

A new site on a large scale with flights, hotels, car hire, destination information, a brochure database, and a travel magazine. It looks good but can sometimes be slow to navigate (and it crashed several times when we last tried it). It was launched in September 1999 by Miller Freeman, the publishers of Travel Trade Gazette, one of the principal weekly trade papers for UK travel agents. Miller Freeman operate the site for the owners, United News & Media plc. This is what is called a 'department store' site in which travel agents and operators can set out their own stands, or at least take out advertising. So, for example, the bookstore is operated by travelbookstore, villa hire is operated by Private Villas, and the flights section is operated by Airline Network.

Information supplied by the Travel News Organisation
...www.travel-news.org

TEN TOP TRAVEL TIPS AS ADVISED BY THE BABYDIRECTORY
www.babydirectory.com

This website includes everything for pregnant women, babies and children, including local information about most of the UK (growing all the time), nanny agencies, nearly new clothes and equipment, free medical advice, breastfeeding counsellors, bookshop. It offers impartial reviews and advice, thousands of listings of useful addresses etc, as well as features on various baby-related topics. It also has a 'best of online shopping' section. The ten top tips are:

1. Do it, especially while they are under two. You pay hardly anything and babies are more adaptable than children.
2. On long flights, pre-book a bulkhead seat.
3. If travelling to developing countries, pack nappies and baby's favourite formula if not breastfeeding.
4. Try to keep breastfeeding, as it is so much easier to have sterile food on tap on demand.
5. Keep a survival bag with you in case you lose all your luggage or are hugely delayed (which you will be), with enough nappies etc to last you.
6. Take a medical kit with sterilising tablets for drinks, sunscreen, Dioralyte for dehydration, Calpol.
7. Get a good backpack so you can walk around with free hands and don't have to fight with a buggy on rough ground.
8. Take enough toys, books and 'cuddlies', including old favourites and new discoveries. Not too much though – remember you have to carry them there and back.
9. Take out good travel insurance.
10. Relax and enjoy it.

Additional baby websites which I have used and found helpful and easy to follow are:
motherandbaby.co.uk – advice on travelling with babies
thebabyregistry.co.uk – extensive, everything you need to know about babies and babycare
babyplace.co.uk – another general baby site that might be of use

All are relevant to Dad as well as Mum!

NATIONAL TOURIST OFFICES IN THE UK

These are the contact numbers and e-mails I personally found of use when researching my travels. A very useful website for general and up to date travel information is www.travel-news.org which is edited by the travel editor of Classic FM, Alastair McKenzie.

Antigua & Barbuda	www.turq.com/antigua	020 7486 7073
Australia	www.aussie.net.au	0990 022000
New South Wales		020 7887 5003
Northern Territories		020 8944 2992
Queensland	www.qttc.com.au	020 8780 2227
South Australia		020 8944 5375
Victoria	www.tourism.vic.gov.au	020 7240 7176
Austria	www.austria-tourism.at	020 7629 0461
Bahamas	www.gobahamas.com	01483 448900
Barbados		020 7636 9448
Belgium		
Brussels & Ardennes		0906 302 0245*
Brussels & Flanders		0891 887799*
Bermuda	www.bermudatourism.com	020 7771 7001
British Virgin Islands		020 7240 4259
Canada	www.canadatourism.com	0891 715000*
Quebec	www.tourisme.gouv.qc.ca	020 7233 8011
Cayman Islands	www.caymanislands.ky	020 7491 7771
China		020 7935 87/9427
Croatia	www.htz.hr	020 8563 7979
Curaçao	www.curacao-tourism.com	020 7431 4045
Cyprus		020 7569 8800
Czech Republic		020 7291 9925
Denmark	www.visitdenmark.com	020 7259 5958
Dominican Republic	www.ios.uk.com/domrep	020 7242 7778
Dubai	www.dubaitourism.com	020 7839 0581
Egypt	interoz.com/egypt	020 7493 5282
Falkland Islands		020 7222 2542
Finland	www.mek.fi	020 7930 5871
France	www.franceguide.com	0891 244123*
Gambia		020 7376 0093
Germany	www.germany-tourism.de	020 7317 0908

Gibraltar	www.gibraltar.gi	020 7836 0777
Greece		020 7734 5997
Grenada	www.grenada.org	020 7370 5164/5
Guatemala		020 7349 0346
Hong Kong	www.hkta.org	020 7533 7100
Hungary		020 7823 1055
Iceland	www.icetourist.is	020 7388 5346
India	www.indiatouristoffice.org	020 7437 3677
Ireland	www.ireland.travel.ie	020 7493 3201
Israel	www.infotour.co.il	020 7299 1111
Italy	www.piuitalia2000.it	020 7408 1254
Jamaica	www.jamaicatravel.com	020 7224 0505
Japan		020 7734 9638
Jersey	www.jersey.gov.uk	020 7630 8787
Jordan	www.jordan-online.com	020 8877 0554
Kenya		020 7355 3144
Korea (South)	www.knto.or.kr	020 7321 2535
Lebanon	www.lebanon-tourism.gov.lb	020 7409 2031
Luxembourg	www.luxembourg.co.uk	020 7434 2800
Macau	www.macau.gov.mo	020 7771 7006
Malawi		0115 982 1903
Malaysia		020 7930 7932
Malta	www.tourism.org.mt	020 7292 4900
Mauritius		020 7584 3666
Mexico	www.mexico-travel.com	020 7499 8586
Monaco		0500 006114**
Morocco		020 7437 0073
Namibia		020 7636 2924
Netherlands	www.visitholland.com	0891 717777*
New Zealand	www.purenz.com	020 7930 1662
Northern Ireland	www.ni-tourism.com	01232 231221
Norway	www.norway.org.uk	020 7839 2650
Philippines		020 7835 1100
Poland	www.poland.pl	020 7580 6688
Portugal	www.portugal.org	020 7494 1441
Seychelles	www.seychelles.uk.com	020 7224 1670
Singapore	www.travel.com.sg/sog	020 7437 0033
Slovenia		020 7734 4630
South Africa		020 8944 8080

South Pacific Tourism Council		020 8876 1938
Spain		020 7486 8077
Sri Lanka		020 7930 2627
St Kitts & Nevis		
	www.interknowledge.com/stkitts-nevis	020 7376 0881
St Lucia		020 7431 3675
St Vincent		
& the Grenadines	www.vincy.com	020 7937 6570
Sweden	www.visit-sweden.com	020 7724 5868
Switzerland	www.switzerlandtourism.ch/uk	020 7734 1921
Thailand	www.tourismthailand.org	020 7499 7679
Tunisia	www.tourismtunisia.co.uk	020 7224 5561
Turkey		020 7355 4207
Turks & Caicos	www.mki.ltd.uk	020 8350 1017
USA (Visit USA)		0900 1600530
California		020 7405 4746
Florida		020 7630 6602
Florida Keys		01564 794555
Georgia		0121 445 4554
Maryland		01295 750789
Massachusetts	www.mass-vacation.com	020 7978 5233
Texas		020 7978 5233
Vermont		020 7836 7190
Virginia		020 8651 4743
Washington DC		020 8877 4521
US Virgin Islands	www.usvi.net	020 7978 5262
Zambia		020 7589 6343
Zimbabwe		020 7240 6169

Calls charged at premium rate
** *Freephone*
Information supplied by the Travel News Organisation
www.travel-news.org

NOTES

NOTES